The Alexander Antidote

*Turning Conflict into a Prescription of
Wholeness for the Local Church*

Dr. Thomas S. Warren II

iUniverse, Inc.
Bloomington

The Alexander Antidote
Turning Conflict into a Prescription of Wholeness for the Local Church

iUniverse books may be ordered through booksellers or by contacting:

iUniverse
1663 Liberty Drive
Bloomington, IN 47403
www.iuniverse.com
1-800-Authors (1-800-288-4677)

Because of the dynamic nature of the Internet, any web addresses or links contained in this book may have changed since publication and may no longer be valid. The views expressed in this work are solely those of the author and do not necessarily reflect the views of the publisher, and the publisher hereby disclaims any responsibility for them.

Any people depicted in stock imagery provided by Thinkstock are models, and such images are being used for illustrative purposes only.

Certain stock imagery © Thinkstock.

ISBN: 978-1-4620-2552-7 (sc)
ISBN: 978-1-4620-2558-9 (hc)
ISBN: 978-1-4620-2553-4 (e)

Printed in the United States of America

iUniverse rev. date: 05/25/2011

Contents

Introduction

As I walked across the stage to receive my diploma, a feeling of anticipation and excitement came over me. After four years in the classroom, I was finally going to enter the real world of ministry. Certainly, I thought, the people of my first church would be excited about me coming too.

I realize now that the feelings I had on that day were normal, but after thirty-five plus years of pastoral ministry and working with pastors and church leaders on a daily basis on conflict resolution, these feelings have been tempered by a big dose of reality. No pastor or church leader should be surprised at what happened next.

My excitement began to wear off as I found myself in the middle of everyday ministry. Unfortunately, I did not know how valuable even a few years of experience would be for me when the time came to deal with the problems that arose in ministry.

Throughout the last thirty-five years, I have discovered that many pastors are unable to cope effectively with the problems they face on a regular basis in the pastorate. I don't mean to imply that the pastorate is without many rewards, however it can also be very challenging. Nevertheless, it is often through these types of experiences that some of the most valuable lessons of life and ministry can be learned. I have often said that the ministry would be great if it weren't for people. The truth is that quite often the best and worst parts of the ministry are often found when dealing with people.

The Best and Worst Case Scenario

People come in all kinds of shapes, sizes, and colors. While there are many differences to be found among the people of the world, amazing similarities can be identified as well. The extent of their similarities or differences usually depends on the context of ministry. When a pastor enters the local church ministry, he cannot always predict the impact a person might have on the ministry, but he can be certain that it will happen.

People can be the source of joy as well as heartache for the pastor. The joy that comes through a meaningful relationship is one of the richest blessings. On the other hand, people can say and do things that can crush a spirit or destroy a dream. One soon learns that it takes a lot of hard work to build a healthy relationship, even within the boundaries of the church. In today's society, one might get the impression that building strong relationships is important, as seminars and books abound on the subject. However, despite these efforts, people regularly express the need for help in their relationships. History suggests that we still have much to learn. Countries continue to be at war over issues because of leaders that are unable or unwilling to negotiate mutual concerns. Communities are split with neighbor against neighbor since we haven't taken the time to get to know each other. Divorce is at an all-time high, often times due to the simple fact that couples do not communicate, and the problems go on and on.

It is true that relationship building is challenging, especially if someone involved is what one might call a "difficult" person. Some have asked me questions like, "Where does a difficult person come from?" and "Why are some people so difficult to work with?" Obviously, a person who is difficult for me might not be so difficult for you. Regardless, for simplicity sake, let me say that a person is difficult when he or she demonstrates at least one of the following characteristics: *a negative spirit, a bad attitude, a continued lack of cooperation, an unwillingness to work toward resolving mutual problems, a you versus me mentality, or the pushing of a personal agenda over against the consensus of a group.*

Difficult people are not absent from the church either. Clergy and laity alike have testified to the destructive efforts of people who expect things to go their way. Those leaders, especially pastors who have tried to cope with the presence of a difficult person, have discovered that the outcome is not always good.

Why does this happen? Why do we find ourselves in these kinds of predicaments? How can we get at the heart of understanding the dynamics of working with people in ways that will benefit everyone? Perhaps we need to understand that our pattern of working with people begins long before the actual encounter.

Misconceptions: The Plague of the Ministry

Growing up in a Christian home played a significant role in the formation of my values and perspectives on life. In an unsuspecting kind of way, it also provided an environment for the nurturing of misconceptions concerning the future. Misconceptions about ministry are often grown in this kind of guarded environment and eventually face a stern challenge to the realities of life and ministry faced by a pastor.

The memories of my first years in the pastorate are still clear in my mind. The dreams I had in the classroom were quickly tested by the demands of the ministry. As the years went on, I discovered that some of the misconceptions I had about life in the pastorate tended to follow me unless adequately dealt with. I guess that there is always the temptation to think that the next place of ministry will be different. Unfortunately, this is not the case. That you escaped the workings of your last difficult person or situation does not take away the possibility of meeting another one in your new setting. Maybe the next one will even be worse!

For this reason alone it would be wise for each pastor to learn to deal with the problem at hand. Where, then, should one turn for help concerning this need? Without question, the Christian leader or pastor must turn to the Word of God. One might ask, "Does the Bible say anything about dealing with difficult people, and, if so, where?"

Biblical Principles

The Bible has a great deal to say about dealing with difficult people. In fact, Paul the Apostle writes the book of Second Timothy in an attempt to warn his young apostolic delegate to be careful in the handling of his difficult person named Alexander (2 Timothy 4:14–15). Alexander had become a poison to Timothy and the church in Ephesus. His behavior had caused much personal distress and havoc in the church. For Timothy's work to go forward in Ephesus, something had to be done. Paul's first step toward resolving this dilemma apart from dealing with his own relationship with Alexander[1] was to inform Timothy of Alexander and warn him of his potential opposition. Nestled within Paul's closing remarks to Timothy (2 Timothy 4) we find these words:

> *Alexander the metal worker did me a great deal of harm. The*

---

1   See Hebrews 12:14–15. Knowing Paul's character, which is based on his New Testament writings, it is safe to assume that Paul had tried to put into practice the advice of the writer to the Hebrews. Paul gives similar advice to Timothy in 2 Timothy 2:22–24.

Lord will repay him for what he has done. You too should be on your guard against him, because he strongly opposed our message.[2]

Identifying Alexander was not a problem. This is often the case when dealing with a difficult person. Eventually his or her behavior becomes noticeable. In this case, when Paul told Timothy to remain behind in Ephesus[3] it was for the sole purpose of dealing with a group of people who were known for stirring up controversy rather than God's work. It is almost certain that Alexander was a member of this group (1 Timothy 1:20).

Even though Timothy would know his adversary, dealing with him in an appropriate manner both for his sake and the church would be his most formidable challenge. Fortunately, for Timothy and for you and me, he had the counsel of the apostle Paul, a wise and faithful veteran of the faith. Together, they would confront the problem and seek to bring the church back to wholeness.

This passage (2 Timothy 4:14–15) is often overlooked in the telling of Paul's story concerning the ministry in Ephesus. Yet, after further consideration, its significance cannot be overstated. Alexander had become a ministerial "thorn in the flesh" for Paul and now Timothy. However, through careful consideration, he can become a *prescription for wholeness* for anyone seeking to understand how to deal with a difficult person in the ministry of the church.

A Prescription for Wholeness

When a person goes to the doctor it is usually because they have noticed certain symptoms. A visit to the doctor will usually result in the doctor prescribing a particular way of treating the illness. It is primarily the responsibility of the patient to carry out the doctor's orders to ensure that the healing process takes place. Failure to follow the doctor's directions can result in extreme sickness, even death.

In the same way, when a church is diagnosed as being sick, it is usually because certain symptoms have been identified. In an attempt to bring healing to the church, people usually turn to the pastor for a proper understanding of what's going on in the church to make it sick. After a close examination of the problem, the pastor will usually prescribe a plan for dealing with the problem. If the church desires to be healed, it is expected that the church will

2   2 Timothy 4:14–15 (New International Version)
3   1 Timothy 1:3–4

agree to the plan and take the appropriate steps to ensure a return to health. This, however, is not always the case.

In reality, some patients need even further assistance in treating their sickness. As in the case of a person, it is not enough to simply talk about what the patient should do to get well. Sometimes, it is absolutely necessary to intervene in the life of the sick person and help him get well.

This appears to have been the need in Ephesus. Paul had ministered in Ephesus for three years (Acts 19:8,10; 20:31) and taught them sound doctrine (1 Timothy 1:11), yet the church was spiritually sick[4] and filled with difficult people. Paul, unable to continue his work in Ephesus personally, sent young Timothy to bring healing by providing the antidote.[5] Timothy's work in Ephesus was intended to be a prescription for wholeness.

By studying the books of 1 and 2 Timothy, along with other relevant biblical passages, a pastor can discover a prescription for wholeness consisting of a series of guidelines and principles used by Paul and other New Testament leaders to deal with difficult people. By following these guidelines and principles, any pastor or leader can begin to identify the problem and move any church toward resolution and healing.

A Concise Statement of Theology

A pastor who fails to realize that effectively dealing with people is an indispensable part of the ministry will soon find himself in a precarious situation. At times he will be tempted to think that sound doctrine alone will solve his problems, even those of an interpersonal nature. However, I have discovered that to deal with a difficult person, a leader needs more than doctrinal purity.

Doctrine is extremely important, and there will be times when a pastor is faced with a situation where he must make a choice between taking a stand for God's truth or pleasing people.[6] But, in the end, God's truth must be regarded as supreme. Yet there are times in a leader's relationship with a person that

---

4   1 Timothy 1:6; 2 Timothy 2:16–18; 3:15.

5   William Morris, (Ed.). *The American Heritage Dictionary of the English Language*, (New York, NY: American Publishing Co., and Houghton Mifflin Co., 1969), pg. 57. Here the antidote is defined as "remedy or other agent to counteract the effects of a poison." Timothy's role in Ephesus was somewhat like an antidote. He was urged to stay in Ephesus to counteract the disease of false teaching and unacceptable behavior going on in the church.

6   In my third pastorate (located in Oregon), I was brought to this point in my ministry. I was faced with a group of people who did not believe in the deity of Christ. I reached a point where I could no longer pastor the church even though I cared very deeply for the people. In this case, doctrine was most important.

to reach him with the essence of the gospel, doctrine will take a back seat to lovingly and truthfully confronting the person.

Paul realized that God's truth and right living must go together. Since Paul knew that God often used doctrine as an instrument to bring about change in the lives of people, he offered these words of advice to his young co-laborer:

> *Watch your life and doctrine closely. Persevere in them, because if you do, you will save both yourself and your hearers[7]*

It is very possible for a leader to have sound doctrine and lose the privilege of being heard due to the way he treats people. Apparently, Paul understood this basic truth:

> *Those who oppose him (the leader) he must gently instruct in the hope that God will grant them repentance leading to a knowledge of the truth, and that they will come to their senses and escape from the trap of the devil, who has taken them captive to do his will.[8]*

Paul was able to see that it was possible to work successfully with a difficult person. In some cases, when a pastor or leader is patient and offers godly instruction, a difficult person will change for the good. On the other hand, it is sometimes necessary to exercise a carefully thought out plan of discipline with the person. The goal in either case is reconciliation and restoration.

What Now?

In the introduction, I have established the importance of:

- Recognizing the presence of difficult people in the pastoral setting.
- Reconstructing any misconceptions one might have about the role that a difficult person can play in the ongoing work of the church.
- Reviewing the Bible's teaching on how one can deal with a difficult person.

---

7   1 Timothy 4:13–16, NIV.
8   2 Timothy 2:25–26, NIV.

- Realizing the potential of the Church when pastors/leaders learn how to deal effectively with difficult people.

In chapter one, I explore the first step in the process of dealing with a difficult person. This chapter will deal with topics such as:

- Gaining a general understanding of the environment out of which a difficult person emerges.
- Developing better recognition skills that enable one to see the most common behavioral tendencies of a difficult person.
- Having a clearer perception of the type of leadership skills needed when dealing with a difficult person.
- Possessing a basic understanding of the types of intervention that can be used when dealing with a difficult person.

Chapters two and three take a close look at the New Testament books of 1 and 2 Timothy from an exegetical perspective. Through a careful study of these texts, one can discern the way in which the apostle Paul advised young Timothy to deal with his difficult person. This material will reveal the importance of:

- Understanding the dynamics of preparing oneself for effective confrontation.
- Balancing one's perceptions with the reality of a situation.
- The importance of exercising patience in a situation of conflict.
- The significance of prayer when dealing with conflict.

Chapter four expands upon the study in 1 and 2 Timothy to include other relevant New Testament passages that shed light on this most important task of the pastor. Working with a difficult person is a task that cannot be overlooked in terms of its importance for church health. The reluctance of any pastor or leader to do so will undoubtedly open the door to further conflict and strife.

In the final section of the book, I have provided a study guide for use in the local church. A pastor, along with his leadership team, will find this helpful as they seek to deal with the presence of conflict in a proactive manner. The use of this study guide is not something that should be rushed. Rather, by working through the material in a prayerful and biblical way, much of the harmful conflict impacting churches today could be avoided.

The purpose of this book is to take a biblical and practical look at conflict resolution by offering some fresh and simple thoughts on how a leader can help resolve conflict that is caused by a difficult person, while continuing to lead the church body forward into effective and healthy ministry.

If you are ready to make a difference in the life of your church and allow the Lord to make an impact through you as you serve Him, even when dealing with a difficult person, then *The Alexander Antidote* is for you. Now is the time for each of us, especially those in leadership positions, to set our minds and hearts to the task of bringing health to the body of Christ whenever it is needed, even if it means dealing with conflict.

Chapter One
Understanding the Problem

The Great Commission was given by Jesus on four different occasions.[9] The most memorable and certainly the most quoted is the one recorded in Matthew's gospel account (Matthew 28:19–20). It is here that we find not only what the disciples were expected to do after Jesus' departure, but also the way in which they were supposed to carry out the Lord's command.

For most, the Great Commission is obeyed by preaching the gospel to all nations. Others, however, suggest that the fulfillment of the Great Commission is only completed when believers become disciples. A disciple in this context is a person who not only believes in the person of Christ but lives faithfully according to his Word "teaching them to obey all that I have commanded you" (Matthew 28:20, NIV).

Still others argue that the Great Commission is fully obeyed when we establish individual churches that can carry on the work of evangelism and discipleship.[10] If planting churches is the biblical criteria for determining whether or not the gospel is being brought to the world, then it would appear that the disciples were successful in their evangelistic venture, particularly in light of the number of churches in today's society.

The church is seemingly everywhere. In virtually every community,

---

9   See John 20:21; Mark 16:15; Matthew 28:19–20; and Luke 24:46–48.

10   C. Peter Wagner, *Church Growth: State of Art*, (Wheaton, IL: Tyndale House Publishers, Inc., 1986), p. 143. In chapter 14, entitled, "The Great Commission and Church Planting," noted church growth expert Elmer Towns states: "The Great Commission implies that church planting is the primary method to evangelize the world. To reach lost people in every culture a church must be established in every culture to communicate the gospel and nurture those who are saved."

regardless of the size of the town or city, a church can be found. Some places have more churches than others;[11] yet, finding a church in most locations is never a difficult task. This is also true in areas where church attendance is significantly low.[12]

While each of these interpretations offers insight into an understanding of the Great Commission, an additional thought is worth consideration. Gerber suggests that a two-fold task is presented in the New Testament's Great Commission regarding the fulfillment of Christ's command: (1) To make responsible, reproducing Christians, and, (2) To make responsible, reproducing churches.[13]

The strategy of planting churches wherever the gospel was preached was apparently a normal practice for the apostles Paul, Barnabas, Silas, and Timothy.[14] Their work in carrying out this strategy suggests a more balanced interpretation of the Great Commission's primary purpose, namely (1) to preach the gospel in order for people to be saved, and (2) to organize them into an active body of believers called the local church.

The practice of planting churches continues to this day. According to one research report,[15] there were over 150 Protestant denominations and at least 325,000 local congregations in America as of 1990. Nevertheless, despite the plethora of churches on the American scene, they are not as visible as one might think. George Barna, a noted researcher of church life in America, states:

> *The name recognition of the average church is lower than might be expected. Fewer than one out of every five people, on the*

---

11   Some cities have a great number of churches. For example, Jacksonville, FL, which has a population of 650–700,000 (1990 census), recently counted over 900 churches within the city limits. This breaks down to 777 people per church if all were in church. Obviously, not all of the people are church attenders. Nevertheless, 900 churches spread over a city's geographical area is significant.

12   In 1988, while I was living in the Northwest section of the United States (Portland, OR), it was reported that Oregon and Washington respectively were the #1 and #2 unchurched states in the country. Yet these two states were filled with churches, big and small. In fact, Portland, OR, was noted for some very large churches that had received international recognition for the ministries.

13   Vergil Gerber, *God's Way To Keep a Church Going and Growing*, (Glendale, CA: Regal Books, 1973), p. 18.

14   See the following biblical tests for an account of Paul's missionary journeys: Acts 13–14; Acts 15:36–18:22; Acts 18:23–21:16

15   *Churches in America as of February 1990*. Arlington, TX: American Church Lists, February 1990.

average, are aware of the existence of the typical church located within their community.[16]

This fact alone raises an extremely important question: What is, or is not, going on inside the churches of America that prevents them from making a significant impact on their communities? The suggestion that this has been the condition of the church is hinted at by George Barna in his book *The Frog in the Kettle*, where he identifies ten critical, achievable goals for the church as it faces the 1990s.[17] It is very interesting to note that at least six of Barna's lists of ten goals pertain directly to the fulfillment of the Great Commission.[18]Apparently, something is blocking the ability of the church to reach these goals. A closer look at the local church and its dynamics provides the answer.

Understanding the First Century Church

The apostles were obviously dedicated to planting churches as a result of the Great Commission. The mere presence of so many churches throughout the apostolic world shows us that this part of the Lord's command was taken very seriously. However, in order to understand more clearly why the church today is not having the impact on the world that God intended, we must take a closer look at the daily life of the church.

Thankfully, the apostle Paul and other New Testament writers cared enough about their newly planted churches to communicate with them regarding the ongoing ministry of the church. Fortunately, this communication included those things that needed praise,[19] as well as the issues that had become problems for the believers.[20]

The pastoral letters of 1 and 2 Timothy provide excellent examples of what can happen when a church is planted and the ministry of the church is blocked. In these letters, Paul gives advice to his young apostolic delegate on

---

16 George Barna, *The Frog in the Kettle*, (Ventura, CA: Regal Books, 1990), p. 130.

17 Ibid., 226–230.

18 Barna's list includes: 1) Win People to Christ, 2) Raise Bible Knowledge, 3) Equip the Christian Body, 4) Establish Christian Community, 5) Renew Christian Behavior, 6) Enhance the Image of the Local Church, 7) Champion Christian Morals, 8) Live By a Christian Philosophy, 9) Restore People's Self-Esteem, and 10) Focus on Reaching the World for Christ. Note particularly numbers 1, 3, 4, 5, 8, and 10 as those relating to the completion of the Great Commission.

19 Colossians 1:3–6.

20 1 Timothy 1:6–11.

how to handle problems that arise in the course of the ministry. By examining these epistles, one will not only discover the types of problems that can arise in ministry, but what can be done in order to ensure that God's work goes on despite the presence of conflict.

The Church at Ephesus

Paul had just been released from prison in Rome (apparently after Acts 28), and had made his way back to the church in Ephesus.[21] His intent was to move on and visit other churches as well as continue his evangelistic work. Unfortunately, the ministry at Ephesus had taken a turn for the worse. Paul, intent on going to Macedonia, was deeply concerned about the church and left young Timothy in charge.

The church at Ephesus, as Timothy soon discovered, was filled with problems. Almost immediately he encountered men and women who opposed the "sound doctrine" (1 Timothy 1:11) that Paul had taught in Ephesus for three years (Acts 20:31). The false teaching that was present in Ephesus at this time soon began to make itself known in a variety of ways: (1) women began to function outside of their God-ordained roles with no respect for their husbands or men in general (1 Timothy 2:8–15); (2) the false teachers started to advocate a lifestyle contrary to the normal relationship between a husband and wife (1 Timothy 4:1–5); (3) young women were being led astray by their own lust (1 Timothy 5:11), men used seductive logic in order to fulfill their own selfish needs (2 Timothy 3:6–7); (4) believers were bringing accusations against their leaders (1 Timothy 5:19); (5) and people were beginning to place an unhealthy emphasis upon money versus contentment through godliness. These distortions of God's truth, as well as many others, ultimately caused the faith of many people in Ephesus to be "shipwrecked" (1 Timothy 1:19).

The ministry in Ephesus was becoming a major responsibility for Timothy.

---

21   This is only one possible viewpoint regarding the life of Paul following the happenings in Acts 28. Another possibility for Paul's experience following his imprisonment in Rome, which is recorded in Acts 28, is that the experience in the Pastoral epistles (see 2 Timothy 4:16, "At my first defense … ") refers to what JND Kelly identifies in his commentary as "primo action" (i.e., primary investigation). JND Kelly, *A Commentary on The Pastoral Epistles: I & II Timothy & Titus*, (Guilford, London and Worcester: Billings & Sons Limited, 1963), p. 216ff. For a brief consideration of the most common viewpoints (strengths and weaknesses) please refer to F.F. Bruce, *Commentary on the Book of Acts*, (Grand Rapids, MI: Wm. B. Eerdmans Publishing Co.,, 1954) and I Howard Marshall, *The Acts of the Apostles: An Introduction and Commentary*, (Grand Rapids, MI: William B. Eerdmans Publishing Co., 1980).

He was not only responsible for dealing with a variety of problems in Ephesus, but he was discovering that problems are sustained by people who strongly support the issues at stake and have definite reasons for their viewpoints. Paul was already aware of certain men in Ephesus who would most likely give Timothy a hard time in the ministry. In particular, he knew of one Alexander who was almost certainly going to cause trouble by opposing his work and the message of Christ (2 Timothy 4:14–15).

It is not quite certain how much time Timothy spent in Ephesus. However, it seems safe to say that the majority of his time was not spent in an evangelistic ministry, but rather in solving problems. Much effort was obviously given to dealing with difficult people who for various reasons opposed "sound doctrine" and all that it represents.

Fortunately, Timothy's experience in Ephesus provides us with a valuable lesson about the pastoral ministry. Sometimes, ministry cannot move forward as desired because leaders have to spend an enormous amount of time dealing with petty issues and difficult people. The end result is obvious. The Great Commission cannot be carried out effectively when leaders are burdened with this type of work.

Understanding the Twenty-first Century

— *The Contemporary Pastor*

Noticeably, things have not changed much in almost two thousand years. In the same way that Timothy faced the challenges of the ministry many years ago, pastors of today are continually confronted with obstacles that prevent them from effectively carrying out the ministry of the church. As in Timothy's experience, the modern day pastor also struggles to maintain a balance between promoting the spiritual maturity of believers in the church while he battles the immaturity of believers who are opposed to any ministry effort that contradicts their own views, feelings, and convictions.

— *The Contemporary Church*

The church of today is very much like the first century church. Despite the differences that one might expect to find between the two, there are many common characteristics that should be considered when one takes a closer look at the ministry of the church.

The first recognizable similarity between the first and twenty-first century churches relates to culture. Each church functions within a given culture. Any attempt to understand the church must take into consideration the role of culture and its influence on the church. But what exactly is culture, and how does it make a difference in the ministry of the church?

In essence, the **culture** of a society may be primitive or advanced. In either circumstance, "the term culture includes the totality of the life pattern—language, religion, literature, machines and inventions, arts, crafts, architecture and decor, dress, laws, customs, marriage and family structures, government and institutions, plus the peculiar and characteristic ways of thinking and acting."[22]

Society is defined as "a self-perpetuating group who share a geographical territory and a culture."[23] In view of these definitions, culture and society can be seen as dependent terms. A culture can be broken down into smaller units when one considers the fact that within societies there are often smaller groups that are similar in many ways to the larger society yet distinguishable from it. These smaller groups are called **subcultures**.[24] Within these subcultures a person learns how to behave in a given situation and eventually expects other members of that society to behave the same way. These expected patterns of behavior are called **norms**.[25]

It is not uncommon for norms to develop within the church.[26] However, the work of recognizing norms that exist within a particular ministry situation is not always easy. Because of this difficulty, a close examination of the subcultures that are significant in the development and growth of a local church, as well as those that hinder growth, is needed. By carefully examining the subcultures within the church, a pastor can begin to comprehend how an issue can be perceived as important, and, in some situations, how a person can become difficult to work with in the local church ministry.

Pastoral experience suggests that at least five subcultures[27] exist within the local church (**historical, familial, pastoral, theological, and geographical/ sociological**). In order to understand the relationship between the issues that

---

22   Richard S. Taylor, *A Return to Christian Culture*, (Minneapolis, MN: Bethany Fellowship, Inc., 1973), p. 12.

23   Ibid., 48.

24   Ibid, 49–50.

25   Ibid, 48–49.

26   Stephen A. Grunlan and Milton Reimer (Eds.), *Christian Perspectives on Sociology*, (Grand Rapids, MI: Zondervan Publishing Co., 1982), p. 48–49. According to Grunlan, sociologists have discovered that there are at least five basic functions in a society around which norms may be clustered: 1) Family, 2) Economics, 3) Government, 4) Education, and 5) Religion.

27   Based on Grunlan's definition of culture (see footnote 18), the term "subculture" is applicable to the church. However, I prefer the phrase, *"contexts of influence"* (italics and phrase mine) due to the fact that it conveys more precisely the impact of these communities on the life of the church.

arise in the ministry setting and the people who hold them, these subcultures must be appreciated for their impact on the church. In the next few pages, I provide a closer examination of each subculture in an attempt to demonstrate its significance.

– *Historical Subculture*

History is more than facts printed on paper. It includes people, experiences, and memories of the past that are desperately in need of interpretation. A proper interpretation will not come easily, but when it does come, it will provide considerable insight into the happenings of today.

The interpretation of history is essential for the modern day pastor. Without an understanding of his local church's history, the pastor will be left to draw conclusions about the church based solely on suspicion and the assistance of selected personal experiences. A careful examination of a local church's history is likely to reveal some interesting and very helpful pieces of information about the church's past pattern of ministry. With these in mind, the pastor can begin to build a better understanding of the present.

– *Familial Subculture*

Therapists today are discovering more than ever the importance of the family, particularly the family of the past. Marriage and family therapist David Field writes:

> *Our present lives are attached to our previous families as if by an umbilical cord. Our behavior and thoughts, our attitudes and reactions, and our values and beliefs are all linked to the family from which we came. Our conscious and unconscious actions and attitudes are tied to what I call our families of origin.*[28]

The family of origin is the home in which a person is raised. Identifying it is easy for some and more difficult for others (e.g., because of high divorce and remarriage rate, etc.) since the family is dynamic (always changing) and seldom static. One thing, however, is certain. The family of origin is very influential in the formation of a person's life. It is within the context of the family that a person develops life-long skills and perceptions about life.

Growing up in the family of origin, a child is also likely to be trained in a variety of ways. Perhaps the most important way, says Field, is by the meeting

---

28   David Field, *Family Personalities*, (Eugene, OR: Harvest House Publishers, 1988), p. 12.

of two basic needs: **individuality** and **relationship**.[29] Individuality concerns itself with the way a person views himself, while relationship relates to the ability of a person to communicate and get along with others. Each family differs in its ability to meet these needs.

One can imagine the type of person that is developed when there is an imbalance within the family and these needs are not met, or when there is an overemphasis on the meeting of one need versus the other. It has been suggested that there are five "family personalities"[30] found along the continuum between individuality and relationship that contribute both positively and negatively to the meeting of these needs. The family that is imbalanced in its ability to meet these needs can produce a child that will potentially be an adult who is unable to function appropriately in a variety of situations.

Understanding the family background of a difficult person is particularly important for a pastor. An awareness of the specifics concerning his family of origin can help a pastor tremendously when attempting to understand his behavior in a given context.[31]

– *Pastoral Subculture*

Very few people are in a position to influence lives like the pastor. Given the opportunity, the pastor can play a significant role in the life of a family over a period of years. Sometimes a pastor's impact is short-lived. Believing his work to be done, he moves to another ministry site. However, there are situations where a pastor may remain in one place for a long time.[32] The impact of such a ministry is far-reaching.

The impact of a long ministry in one place can be seen in a variety of ways. If the church has had only a few pastors, then a pastor who stays for an extended period of time has the opportunity to make a significant impression upon the hearts and minds of the parishioners. He can influence their thinking in many areas. Over a long period of time a church gets accustomed to the

---

29   Ibid., 25

30   Ibid., 27–28. According to Field, there are five personalities found along the continuum between meeting the needs of individuality and relationship: 1) Bonding, 2) Ruling, 3) Protecting, 4) Chaotic, 5) Symbiotic.

31   Ibid., 29. Here Field suggests that a family personality uniquely expresses certain ingredients: 1) Position on the continuum of individuality and relationship, 2) Marriage relationship of the parents, 3) Parenting style, 4) Children's response to the family personality, 5) Family dynamics— including communication skills, crisis management, and responses to the outside world, 6) Religious influence and values, and 7) Exiting—how the children function as adults.

32   In my own denomination, I am aware of some men who have been in one ministry site for over twenty, thirty, and forty years.

way their pastor dresses, eats, drives, talks, preaches, teaches, visits or doesn't visit, plans, works around the office, vacations, laughs, cries, spends his leisure time, and the list goes on and on. Unfortunately, time has a way of causing people not to take a closer look at the way things are being done until someone comes along and challenges their thinking and behavior.

The fact that a church sometimes tolerates the ways of their leader does not mean that the leader is right. In some cases, leaders have been guilty of misleading their people (e.g., Jim Jones, Jim Bakker) under the pretense of truth. Not all local church ministries can be compared to a large television ministry that goes astray. Nevertheless, it does point out the possibility that people can become so accustomed to a particular way of ministry that it is difficult for them to accept change.

A pastor entering a new ministry often encounters people who are unwilling to accept change. In some situations, people have been taught a certain way for so long that it is virtually inconceivable to them that there might be another point of view that has merit. It may be a theological thought, a point of view on the role of the laity, an opinion about the bulletin and the worship service, or how the pastor spends his spare time. It really doesn't matter. The fact that people have these thoughts and are unwilling to change is enough to cause trouble for any pastor.

The difficult person is the one member who holds these viewpoints to be more precious, more sacred, than others and is willing to fight for them. The pastor who is careful to find out about the history of the pastoral ministry in the church will lay the groundwork for making progress in his own pastoral ministry in the present.

— *Theological Subculture*

A few years ago, while I was teaching a Bible study on the doctrine of Christ, a lady voiced opposition to a particular aspect of the lesson. After discussing the matter for a few minutes, I discovered that she did not believe in the deity of Christ. Obviously, this troubled me, so I asked her why she held this position. Her answer was equally disturbing, but after a great deal of reflection, I understood more clearly why she believed the way she did. She simply said, "Well, that's the way I've always been taught to believe!"

She was exactly right. In her case, she had been in the same church for over forty years, sat under the ministry of several pastors who held this theological position, and most importantly, she had been in a family structure that accepted this teaching to be true and had successfully passed it down through a number of generations. How could she believe anything else?

Likewise, how could my presence not cause a problem when it was discovered that I held a contrary view on the nature of Christ?

This kind of situation is not that uncommon in the local church. Each time a pastor begins a new ministry, he also inherits a long history of theological teaching that may or may not be biblically based. In addition to this, he also inherits certain people who hold these teachings to be absolute truth. A difficult person may emerge from this group due to the fact that he views the new pastor with a different theological position as a threat to his convictions and long-time admiration of those who taught him the Scripture.

For a pastor to be prepared for the task of working with a difficult person, he must have a basic understanding of the theological history of the person and his church.

— *Geographical/Sociological Subculture*

Churches[33] can be found in virtually every kind of setting. Some are located on the main street of a rural town in the northeast corner of the state where life is slow and deliberate. Others can be found in a major metropolitan city on the corner of a busy street that is three blocks from the downtown commercial section or five blocks over from the place where gangs run freely. Still others might be discovered on a dirt road around the bend from the crystal clear creek that has brought refreshment to the people of the area for years. Regardless of where the church is located, it always has meaning to those who live in the community as well as those who are faithful members of the church fellowship.

The church[34] has meaning for most people, but it is not necessarily the same. The variety of views undoubtedly comes from the fact that not all people have an equal amount of contact with the church. Because of this, the beliefs about the significance of the church vary from one community to the next largely in direct proportion to the degree in which people are in contact with the church and understand its intended role.

It is not difficult to see how a person might develop a view of the church from the way in which the church functions within a particular setting. If the church is perceived to be active and involved in the community, a person would most likely begin to think that the church is useful and necessary. On the other hand, if the church is not seen to be involved in the activities and

---

33   The word "church" is used here in terms of the church building. The author recognized that the church is not a building, but people who have been saved by the Lord Jesus Christ.

34   Here the word "church" refers to the group of people who have been saved through Christ.

concerns of the community, a person is more prone to think that the church doesn't care and/or has nothing to offer in the way of solutions.

Encountering people in the church who oppose the pastor's view about the role of the church is not uncommon. However, it may have a lot to do with the fact that these people have grown up in a community of faith where the church has been removed from the needs and issues of the community in which it is located. The church family sees the ministry of the church as something separate but parallel to the happenings of the world. A pastor who understands the history of the local church and its personal view of ministry combined with the attitude of the community toward the church will be helped tremendously in his effort to carry out the ministry.

Conflict comes in a variety of shapes and colors.[35] Being able to determine the shape or color of a particular conflict is an important task for the pastor and must be taken seriously. The first step toward effectively dealing with conflict is understanding. Therefore, it is essential that a pastor understand the five "contexts of influence" (subcultures) that have contributed to the development of the person who has now become difficult. The next step toward resolving conflict and effectively dealing with a difficult person is to understand the person in relationship to the problem.

Underdstanding the Person and His Problem

The local church ministry as we know it today and as it was intended to be by our Lord could not take place without people. In fact, the Great Commission that Jesus gave to his disciples at his departure was people-centered. Nestled within the Great Commission is a command to preach the gospel "to people" and "to reach people" with the essence of the gospel by making disciples (Matthew 28:19–20). The ministry, therefore, is to be primarily concerned with turning people into "Christ Followers."[36] This has never been an easy task and perhaps never will be as long as there is the presence of people.

Why is it so difficult to turn people into Christ Followers? The Bible says it is due to the fact that each man and woman is a sinner who has fallen short of God's expectations (Romans 3:23). As a result, our natural inclination is to

---

35 Edward G. Dobson, Speed B. Leas, and Marshall Shelley, *Managing Conflict and Controversy*, (Portland, OR: Multnomah Press, 1992), p. 83f. In a chapter written by Speed Leas (chapter six), conflict is described in terms of colors: 1) Red-fiery hot: shouting matches, withdrawn pledges, fired pastors, split churches; 2) Blue-cool and calm as a mountain lake: issues are moved, seconded, debated calmly, and voted upon; 3) Green: contributing to the growth of everyone; 4) Black: foreboding doom for the church; 5) Gray: uncertain and undecided.

36 Gordon MacDonald, *Christ Followers in the Real World*, (Nashville, TN: Thomas Nelson Publishers, 1989), p. 10.

please ourselves and not God. Subsequently, becoming like Christ is a daily and constant battle (2 Corinthians 4:7–18) for every believer. In this sense, everyone is the same.

However, people are different. People look at things differently, act differently, talk differently, and think differently. Because people are difficult in these and other ways, a pastor must not only be prepared to work with those who, although saved, continue to express their different opinions and feelings, but also be ready for the variety of ways in which people express their sinfulness. In many situations it is the fact that people are different that makes conflict possible and probable. The pastor who is sensitive to this fact will be better prepared to manage conflict when it arises in the ministry setting.[37]

Regardless of the fact that conflict can take many forms in a ministry, it has been suggested that most conflict is experienced in at least one of three ways or in a combination of three ways:

1. Intrapersonal Conflict: the conflict that one has when different parts of the self compete with one another.

2. Interpersonal Conflict: personality differences between people who are not related primarily to issues.

3. Substantive Conflict: disputes over facts, values, goals, and beliefs.[38]

In the beginning stages, most conflict appears to be focused on some kind of substantive issue. Leas and Kittlaus have identified at least four types of substantive conflict experienced in the church of today:

1. Conflict over facts.

2. Conflict over methods or means.

3. Conflict over ends or goals.

4. Conflict over values.[39]

According to Leas and Kittlaus, the degree to which conflict becomes a problem in the local church depends largely on the people who are in conflict

---

37 William E. Willimon, *Preaching About Conflict in the Church*, (Philadelphia, PA: The Westminster Press, 1987), p. 18. Willimon suggests that wise management of conflict begins with a sensitivity to the potential for conflict.

38 Speed Leas and Paul Kittlaus, *Church Fights: Managing Conflict*, (Philadelphia, PA: The Westminster Press, 1973), p. 29–32.

39 Ibid., 32–34.

with each other. This can be demonstrated through a closer examination of what Speed Leas calls the **five levels of conflict**. Each level's degree of difficulty hinges on the objectives of the party and the way he uses language. The following levels appear in their ascending order of difficulty:

Problems to Solve
Disagreement
Contest
Fight/Flight
Intractable Situations[40]

It is quite clear from the work done by Speed Leas on the levels of conflict that there can be a short transition from having people disagree on a substantive issue to experiencing an "all-out war" where elimination of your foe is the objective. In each of the levels identified, one thing seems clear: the longer two parties are unable to deal with the issue at hand, the more difficult it becomes to deal with the person defending it. Therefore, failure to make satisfactory progress in resolving a conflict hinges largely on a proper understanding of the person(s) you oppose.

Understanding the People in the Ministry Setting

The need to understand people is quite obvious for anyone who has been a part of the pastoral ministry. Eventually, every leader discovers those people, affectionately called by Carl George "E.G.R.'s or Extra Grace Required Persons,"[41] who challenge them in ways they would never have anticipated. Seeking to understand why people behave the way they do is likely to be an ongoing task in the ministry, but not one that can be neglected.

In his book *Well-Intentioned Dragons*, Marshall Shelley suggests at least two reasons why people's behavior often becomes the focus of a problem that exists in the church: (1) people feel so strongly about an issue that their emotions begin to override the facts, and (2) people cannot overcome the effect of their sinful nature.[42]

The church may have a corner on the market when it comes to people who behave in extraordinary ways. This is definitely a possibility, writes Shelley,

---

40   Speed Leas, *Managing Your Church Through Conflict*, (New York, NY: The Alban Institute, 1985), p. 19.

41   John Ortberg, *Leadership*, "Breaking the Approval Addiction," (Carol Stream, IL: Christianity Today Publications, 1992), p. 38.

42   Marshall Shelley, *Well-Intentioned Dragons*, (Ada, MI: Bethany House, 1994), p. 46–48.

when one considers that the church, "unlike some social organizations, doesn't have the luxury of choosing its members; the church is an assembly of all who profess themselves believers. Within that gathering is found a full range of saint/sinner combinations."[43] Nevertheless, declares Shelly, "ministry is a commitment to care for all members of the body, even those whose breath is tainted with dragon smoke."[44]

The nature of the church itself demands that pastors be able to identify and distinguish a well-intentioned dragon from a dragon,[45] in order to work toward resolution of any existing problem. A pastor's inability or unwillingness to do this can only contribute to the problem and stymie the ministry of the church.

Over the years, pastors and church leaders have been able to identify a variety of people within the ministry setting that qualify as difficult. Amazingly, among these leaders there is a tremendous amount of similarity in the types of people who are believed to be potential "dragons." A careful examination of these types of people is essential for the pastor when considering the development of a plan of intervention to deal with the presence of these people. Material has been compiled in order to show the common perception among leaders when it comes to identifying difficult people and their tactics.[46]

Moving Beyond Identification

Difficult people[47] may not be hard to find, but it is extremely challenging to understand their needs and respond to their demands. In fact, every relationship we have with people is, in the words of Judson Edwards, "a collision of two worlds with all their similarities and differences." Edwards writes:

> *We bring to that relationship our own unique world; our*

---

43 Ibid., 48.

44 Ibid., 37.

45 I have used the term "dragon" to describe those people in the church who have moved beyond the point of a simple disagreement to the desire for destroying those whom they oppose and perceives to be in the way of fulfilling their wants.

46 Many authors today provide a wide variety of names and characteristics given to difficult people. For more information, please refer to the work of one or more of the following authors: Rick Brinkman, Robert Dale, William Diehm, Judson Edwards, Kenneth Haugk, Rick Kirschner, and Francis Littauer.

47 Difficult people is only one name given to the people who have caused problems in the pastoral ministry. Other names include: well-intentioned dragons (Marshall Shelley) and antagonists (Kenneth Haugk).

experiences, temperament, family background, religious heritage, style of relating to people, taste for food and music and entertainment, and so on.[48]

Developing the ability to work with difficult people needs to be a high priority for any pastor who wants to be able to carry on the work of the church. Some pastors neglect the task of dealing with a difficult person when a problem arises. Unfortunately, by failing to work toward a satisfactory solution, the pastor and church contribute to the development of a vicious cycle of repeating their problems.

Fortunately, there is hope. Pastors can learn to deal with difficult persons in a constructive manner, and in so doing, make possible the growth and increased effectiveness of the ministry of the church. This process begins when each pastor sees his relationships with difficult people as an opportunity for everyone involved to learn and grow. Again, in the words of Judson Edwards, the relationship becomes an opportunity for a **"tender collision"**:

> *True, no one is from our exact world (which, by the way, always makes them look wrong to us). True, every relationship we have will involve a collision of some sort. But that collision doesn't have to be an abrasive, destructive one. We can learn the art of tender collisions, and in the process learn to love people more.*[49]

Needed: Transforming Leaders

For many, turning a relationship with a difficult person into a "tender collision" is not an easy task. Most of us have come to view conflict as a threat to relationships rather than an encouragement to them. It is often difficult for us to imagine anything positive resulting from discord. This only goes to show how bogged down we have become in our outdated approaches to resolving conflict.

Certainly, no one modeled the art of "tender collisions" better than Jesus. Jesus was well acquainted with conflict. However, whatever the source of controversy, Jesus consistently followed a strategy of conflict resolution that defended both principles and people. At the heart of Jesus' conflict style was a commitment to win people rather than arguments.[50]

---

48 Judson Edwards, *What They Never Told Us About How To Get Along With Each Other*, (Eugene, OR: Harvest House Publishers, 1991), p. 9.

49 Ibid., 10.

50 James Hindle and Tim Woodroof, *Among Friends*, (Colorado Springs, CO:

We too must follow the model of Jesus as we deal with difficult people. In the words of Leighton Ford, we must have leaders who are capable of turning the most inhumane circumstances into situations of hope by the way we choose to react to them. We must become "Transforming Leaders."[51]

The Absence of Leaders

As the church begins the twenty-first century, there is a definite need for leadership. The need extends far beyond the "preaching of the Word" (2 Timothy 4:2). Many pastors are well equipped to deliver sermons that will *encourage, enlighten, and enthusiastically challenge the modern parishioner.* Yet how many pastors are prepared to complete the command given to Timothy in Paul's last letter to his apostolic delegate while he was ministering in Ephesus (2 Timothy 4:15)?

This command involves the preaching of the Word, but much more. Timothy was commanded "keep your head in **all** situations, endure hardship, do the work of an evangelist, discharge **all** the duties of your (his) ministry" (2 Timothy 4:5). Every pastor is aware of those times when more is expected of him than preaching the Word. There comes a time when the truth of the Word must be applied to the lives of people in very practical ways.

The church is in need of leaders who will not only preach the Word, but those who will cause the Word to impact upon the lives of people, particularly those who are considered difficult. The ability to carry out this command comes from two primary sources: (1) the willingness to model the life of Jesus, who always gave himself sacrificially and humbly to other people, and (2) the desire to learn and develop skills that will enable one to intervene in a problem situation and offer hope for a satisfactory resolution.

Much material has been written on the subject of working with difficult people.[52] Unfortunately, it would take a significant amount of time for a person to read all of this material. However, time is a precious commodity for the busy leader who finds himself in need of assistance when attempting to deal effectively with a difficult person. In this book I have provided as a

---

NAVPRESS, 1989), p. 154. In this book, it is argued that Jesus chose a win/ win style of conflict management. However, the scripture also indicates that, on certain occasions, Jesus was so strongly confrontive that it appeared that he didn't concern himself with how people responded (cf. Matthew 23). Nevertheless, even in this passage, Jesus indicates his original longing for the people who ultimately rejected him as Savior (Matthew 23:37).

51 Leighton Ford, *Transforming Leadership*, (Downers Grove, IL: InterVarsity Press, 1991), p. 257.

52 See A Selective Annotated Bibliography on page TK for books and periodicals related to the subject of dealing with difficult people.

guidebook for dealing with the difficult person in the local church. Such a tool will be invaluable to the pastor as he carries out his ministry.

A Workable Plan

The development of a practical strategy for effectively dealing with a difficult person is built upon the belief that such a tool will be helpful in the daily work of the pastor. Anyone who uses such a plan will discover at least five truths regarding the process of working with the difficult person.

> **Truth #1***: It is **helpful** to have in hand a plan of action that is flexible and easily accessible for dealing with the difficult person.*

> **Truth #2***: It is **insightful** to look at conflict from the viewpoints of both pastoral leadership as well as from that of the difficult person. Having a plan that includes this kind of examination of a conflict situation will prove to be valuable.*

> **Truth #3***: It is **beneficial** to have available a plan that takes into consideration factors beyond right and wrong when dealing with conflict. This type of plan will seriously consider the important role of personalities, expectations, etc., all of which contribute to a proper understanding of the difficult person and makes possible wise choices by the pastoral leadership as they seek to minister to the difficult person in the context of the local church ministry.*

> **Truth #4***: It is **advantageous** to the pastoral leadership to have access to a plan of intervention that anticipates many of the possible reactions to intervention and suggests alternative reactions in order to maintain balance and perspective in the midst of conflict.*

> **Truth #5***: It is **comforting** to know that the Bible has a great amount to say about working with those who are considered difficult people. Those who use a plan of intervention will discover the importance of Bible study and prayer when working with the difficult person.*

Criteria and Characteristics

Most pastors/leaders would welcome the development and availability of a workable plan of intervention for dealing with the difficult person. In order for such a plan to be effective, it must be **sound** in doctrine (biblical), **flexible and practical** in use (flexible, informative, and directional), and it must be **realistic** in its interpretation (empathetic, informative, and include closure: bringing conflict to a satisfactory solution and/or conclusion). A closer look at each characteristic will reveal how such a model would be helpful to the pastor who needs assistance in dealing with a difficult person.

– *Biblical*

In an effort to understand how Paul and other biblical leaders deal with the difficult person, and to see more clearly how Jesus dealt with conflict, the pastor must turn to the scriptures. A casual and superficial glance at the Word of God will not provide the spiritual nourishment necessary to take the pastor through a trying situation with a difficult person. A plan that will take a closer look at the way in which Jesus, Paul, and a number of other biblical characters deal with conflict will be an asset to the pastor as he seeks to move the church toward doing God's will in the midst of conflict.

– *Flexible*

Many books have been written about the subject of dealing with difficult people. Each book addresses the subject from its own particular point of view and often suggests that their view is the appropriate perspective. This may or may not be true. The fact that a book looks at an issue from only one point of view does not make the book wrong or unworthy of consideration. Many of the books written on the subject of dealing with difficult people are excellent resources.

The experience of the pastorate has shown that problems do not always fit into a neat little package. Each problem carries with it a multitude of concerns. There is a need today for an approach to dealing with difficult people that has flexibility inherent within its design. A plan of intervention that can bend in relationship to the need would be very useful to the pastor who seeks guidance in the midst of a conflict situation.

– *Informative*

Although a book may do an excellent job of addressing a subject area of interest, it may do so in a tedious fashion. In this day and age people are interested in finding helpful information as quickly as possible, especially when they are confronted with the task of bringing resolution to a problem. Having an intervention plan that makes it easier for a person to get his hands on relevant information in a reasonable amount of time would be extremely helpful.

— *Directional*

In order to deal effectively with conflict, we must have a variety of options when it comes to solving a problem. No two conflict situations are exactly alike, and certainly no two difficult people are the same either. Anyone who suggests that there is only one way to go about solving a problem has not thought very much about the problem.

— *Empathetic*

Conflict resolution is more than theory. It is not enough to simply apply the latest formula in an attempt to deal with a difficult person. People need to feel that they are more than the latest project on a pastor's schedule. A plan of intervention that takes into consideration the feelings of people as well as their position on an issue sends a message of care.

— *Interpretive*

Experience in the pastoral ministry has demonstrated that people behave in certain ways in order to achieve particular goals. An intervention plan that provides information that helps the pastor better understand the varying nature of personality types and behavioral tendencies will go far in enhancing the leader's ability to resolve the conflict.

— *Closure*

The goal of conflict resolution is closure. Each pastor will strive to bring a problem under control and hopefully will find a satisfactory solution for all involved. Sometimes this is not possible. However, it is still important to pursue the best solution possible in light of the situation's complexities. Failure to bring closure to a conflict can lay the groundwork for further problems or at the least a repeat of the same old problem. The next time a problem arises, it may be more serious than when it originally manifested itself.

Implementing a Plan of Action

Dealing with a difficult person is challenging to say the least. It is, however, worthy of our best efforts. Through the development and use of a workable plan, pastors will be given the opportunity to make a difference in the lives of people who are difficult.

Since conflict rarely just happens, it is wise to remember that neither does the resolution of conflict. Therefore, a workable plan of intervention will be an essential tool for the pastor who is concerned with the impact of a difficult person on the life and health of the church.

Finding a workable plan of conflict resolution is a primary task of most pastors. Once a plan is identified, the pastor will be on his way to bringing creative and long-lasting solutions to the problems he faces in the ministry.

Chapter Two
Finding Balance in the Storm

When faced with the task of dealing with a difficult person, most pastors need a plan that will enable them to cope effectively while at the same time managing or carrying on the regular duties of their ministry (2 Timothy 4:5).

The plan must come from the scriptures. The Bible alone must be his primary source of guidance if he seeks to work through problems in a way that is pleasing to the Lord. Fortunately, the Bible offers many insights on this subject.

In the New Testament, the apostle Paul stands out as one who had the experience of working with difficult people. This can be seen through Paul's experience in Ephesus, where he ministered to a man by the name of Alexander, and more importantly his instruction to Timothy about working with people like Alexander. In the books of 1 and 2 Timothy, Paul offers a leader much insight on dealing with the difficult person.

Following Paul's instructions make possible the ongoing work of the ministry and at the same time enables the difficult person and pastor to co-exist in such a way as not to hinder the gospel or harm the people of the ministry. In order to understand Paul's teaching on this subject, a closer look at the text is necessary.

Ephesus: A Ministry in Transition

The ministry in Ephesus was about to change. The apostle Paul, a veteran of the faith, found himself reaching a climatic point in his life. Though his ministry had been filled with a mixture of struggles and blessings, he now faced what might be considered his greatest challenge. Under guard in a

Roman prison and doubtful of his release, Paul penned what is considered by many to be his final correspondence. Regardless of the fact that he had been delivered from the lion's mouth[53] at his first defense, his letter is filled with a sense of personal resignation implying that now more than ever, his death was inevitable.

> *For I am already being poured out like a drink offering, and the time has come for my departure. I have fought the good fight, I have finished the race, I have kept the faith. Now there is in store for me the crown of righteousness, which the Lord, the righteous Judge, will award to me on that day-and not only to me, but also to all who have longed for his appearing.*[54]

At Paul's first defense (2 Timothy 4:16), no one came to his support. Like Demas (2 Timothy 4:9), each of Paul's fellow laborers in the faith had reasons for not being there in his most difficult hour. However, Paul was not left alone in his dilemma. When the Roman believers failed to show up in Paul's defense, the Lord stood by his servant, fulfilling his promise never to leave him (Matthew 10:19).

> *But when they arrest you, do not worry about what to say or how to say it. At that time you will be given what to say, for it will not be you speaking, but the Spirit of your Father speaking through you.*

It is unclear why members of the Roman Christian community with whom he had been very close were not present to give him support.[55] Despite the

---

53 1 Timothy 4:17. The lion's mouth has been taken by some to refer to death in the amphitheater, a common site for Christians who had been sentenced to death. But as a Roman citizen, Paul would most likely have been beheaded. See Ronald A. Ward, *Commentary on 1 & 2 Timothy and Titus*, (Waco, TX: Word Books, 1974), p. 221. Others have suggested that "lion's mouth" refers to Nero, based on the fact that the Greek fathers liked to identify him in this way. See JND Kelly, *A Commentary on the Pastoral Epistles: 1 & 2 Timothy, Titus*, (London, UK: Adam & Charles Black Publishers, 1963), p. 219. But perhaps the most likely interpretation is that the reference to "lion's mouth" refers to a proverbial statement emphasizing extreme danger (see Psalms 7:2; 22:21; 35:17, etc.). In regard to Paul's statement about this being his first defense, see footnote 13 in chapter one for a brief explanation.

54 2 Timothy 4:7–8.

55 2 Timothy 4:16. (Greek παρεγενετο, 3rd person singular 2nd aorist middle

desertion of his friends, God provided him with strength (Gk.ενδυναμοω)[56] sufficient enough to proclaim the gospel with power and effectiveness.[57] Paul was able to complete his God-given task of preaching the gospel due to the grace he had received for this very purpose (2 Timothy 1:9b–11); grace that would ultimately lead Paul to have confidence that God would always be his defender.

> *The Lord will rescue me from every evil attack and will bring me safely to his heavenly kingdom. To him be glory forever and ever. Amen.*[58]

---

indicative of παραγινομαι, to stand with, help). Some have suggested that the reason the believers did not show up to support Paul extended far beyond fear. It is believed that we hear in this word, if only slightly, a hint of division in the Christian community. See JND Kelly, *A Commentary on the Pastoral Epistles: 1 & 2 Timothy, Titus*, (London, UK: Adam & Charles Black Publishers, 1963), P. 218.

56 2 Timothy 4:17. (Greek ενεδυναμωσεν, 3rd person singular aorist active indicative of ενδυναμοω, to strengthen). The context suggests that this is more than physical power or intellectual insight. It suggests spiritual power. A form of this Greek verb is also used in Acts 9:22; Philippians 4:13; I Timothy 1:12; and in 2 Timothy 2:1, with meanings ranging from power, influence, ability, and stamina as well as moral, physical, and spiritual strength.

57 2 Timothy 4:17.

58 2 Timothy 4:18. (Greek παντος εργου πονηρου) translated in the NIV as "every evil attack." See Walter Bauer (transl. by William F. Arndt and F. Wilbur Gingrich), *A Greek-English Lexicon of the New Testament and Other Early Christian Literature*, (Chicago, IL: The University of Chicago Press, 1957), p. 307 (εργου) and p. 697 (πονηρου), for a more detailed discussion of the way εργου, literally "works," is used in the New Testament. See Kenneth S. Wuest, *Word Studies. The Pastoral Epistles in the Greek New Testament for the English Reader*, (Grand Rapids, MI: William B. Eerdmans Publishing Co., 1952), p. 170. Here Wuest argues that the word translated "works/attack" carries with it a subjective reference and suggests an action that would be committed by Paul himself and not some external act (i.e. failure to proclaim the gospel in this situation would have been an "evil work"). The author does not support this interpretation. Rather, it is his belief that Paul is referring to a spiritual rescue, affirming his confidence that no attack of his enemies will undermine his faith or courage. See JND Kelly for a further explanation of this position, p. 220. Although Paul believed that God would rescue him from every evil attack (Greek ρυσεται, 3rd person singular future middle indicative of [ρυομαι], to rescue, save, deliver). He also believed that God would ultimately save (Greek σωσει, 3rd person singular future indicative of [σωζω], to save or preserve)

Paul's confidence in the Lord continued despite his circumstances. Regardless of his imprisonment, Paul was certain that God would continue to carry on the preaching of the gospel. Interestingly enough, the future work of the gospel in Ephesus began a few years earlier in the life of Paul when he visited the city of Lystra (Acts 16:1).

It was in Lystra that Paul met a young disciple named Timothy. Apparently, Timothy had become a believer, along with his mother, during Paul's previous missionary visit to Lystra (Acts 14:1–23; 2 Timothy 1:5) and had made remarkable progress in the faith. So much so that not only did the brothers in Lystra and Iconium speak favorably of Timothy, but Paul too noticed the maturity of his faith and requested that he continue on with him on his missionary journey (Acts 16:1–3).

Paul's decision to take Timothy with him on his journey was not without concern. First, and perhaps most importantly, how would Paul deal with the fact that Timothy was raised Jewish yet his father was a Greek, especially in view of the discussion that had recently taken place at the Jerusalem council (Acts 15:1–35)?[59] At first glance the fact that the people of Lystra and the surrounding area knew of Timothy's mixed parental heritage would appear to be the primary reason that Paul decided to circumcise Timothy before he took him along as his travel companion (Acts 16:3).[60] Even so, Paul's decision to circumcise Timothy was not a violation of his own teaching or the decision of the council, since, even in Galatians, Paul argues that circumcision in itself is religiously indifferent (Galatians 5:6). For Paul, it was a simple matter of expediency. It seems more likely that Paul simply viewed this act alone as a step necessary for Timothy in order to be of greater usefulness in the ministry of the gospel.

Secondly, Paul's endorsement of Timothy was not sufficient. Whatever

---

him into (Greek εἰς) his heavenly kingdom. Whatever happened, God was in control and would take care of Paul.

59   Acts 15:1–35. The final outcome at the Jerusalem council did not require non-Jews to be circumcised. But the fact that the council took place in order to deal with this subject suggests that there were those who thought this should be the standard practice. For an excellent sermon on this passage, see: David Thoms "The Church Faces Conflict." One of four sermons prepared on the subject of conflict in a project for the Doctor of Ministry program at Gordon-Conwell Theological Seminary, South Hamilton, MA, 1986, pp. 25–35.

60   Timothy's mother (Eunice by name, according to 2 Timothy 1:5) married a Greek. See F.F. Bruce for the idea that Timothy's father was dead at this time. He bases this thought on the use of the imperfect tense of υπαρχω (υπηρχεν) in Acts 16:3. For more information concerning the use of this word, see: F.F. Bruce, *The New International Commentary on the New Testament: The Book of Acts*, (Grand Rapids, MI: William B. Eerdman's Publishing Co., 1954), p. 322.

Paul saw in the young disciple at this point in his life was also confirmed by the elders of the church. It seems likely that this was the confirmation experience Paul spoke of in his first letter to Timothy when he exhorted him to live in accordance with the prophecies made about him when the elders laid their hands on him (1 Timothy 1:18; 4:14).

Certain that Timothy was to be with them in ministry, Paul, Silas, and their new companion set out to visit the churches previously established by Paul on his missionary journeys. Now years later, we find Paul revisiting the church at Ephesus only to find that it was in the midst of chaos. Torn between his love for the church and his desire to return to Macedonia,[61] Paul decided to leave his young apostolic delegate Timothy in charge of the ministry at Ephesus (1 Timothy 1:3).

Leaving Timothy in Ephesus was not an easy experience for Paul or Timothy. For years Timothy had been under the guidance of his mentor in the faith, but now the situation had changed. Timothy would be on his own as he tried to deal with the conflict in the church.

Although Paul would not be present physically with him as he ministered in Ephesus, Timothy was constantly on Paul's mind. Each time Paul bowed his head and heart in prayer, Timothy and the need in Ephesus was present.

> *I thank God, whom I serve, as my forefathers did, with a clear conscience, as night and day I constantly remember you in my prayers.*[62]

For Paul, remembering Timothy in prayer was an emotional experience. Recalling the reason he left Timothy in Ephesus (1 Timothy 1:3) and the nature of their last meeting was reason enough for Paul to be filled with a desire to see his fellow servant again.[63]

---

61 This trip into Macedonia does not fit into the journeys that are listed in the book of Acts. Apparently, Paul intended to return to Macedonia near the time that he revisited Ephesus and discovered that the church was experiencing problems. He had no one better than Timothy and no one he trusted more to give leadership to the situation in Ephesus (1 Timothy 1:3).

62 2 Timothy 1:3. Paul demonstrates in this statement and prayer that he saw Timothy as the continuation of his ministry in Ephesus. As one will discover later on in this same passage, Paul had complete confidence in his young apostolic delegate. The same faith Paul had shared with his own ancestors, he now saw in Timothy.

63 2 Timothy 1:4. This reference to the sharing of tears may refer to the parting at Miletus (Acts 20:36–37). The primary difficulty with this interpretation is that this experience is probably, at best, dated years earlier than the experience mentioned in Timothy. Perhaps the best interpretation of this passage is that

Timothy's task of bringing the truth of the scriptures to bear on the false teaching of "certain men" (1 Timothy 1:3) would not be easy. No one, however, knew the ability of this young man better than Paul. The same faith Paul had seen in Timothy's grandmother (Lois) and mother (Eunice), Paul now saw in Timothy.[64]

Paul's conviction about the quality of Timothy's faith did not waver in view of the task that lay before him in Ephesus. Now more than ever, Paul was confident that Timothy possessed the faith[65] and was capable of carrying on the work. For this reason Paul passed on the instruction found in 1 and 2 Timothy in an effort to encourage Timothy to stay true to the pattern of ministry already set by Paul and to counteract what appeared to be a growing problem in the church.

> *Timothy, my son, I give you this instruction in keeping with the prophecies once made about you, so that by following them you may fight the good fight, holding on to faith and a good conscience. Some have rejected these and so have shipwrecked their faith.*[66]

The character of Timothy was unquestionable but nevertheless imperfect. Like many pastors, he too struggled to maintain character that does not bend in the face of adversity.[67] Timothy's character would face its sternest challenge in the hostile environment of Ephesus, as daily he would be called upon to

---

Paul is remembering the experience prior to his second imprisonment in Rome and the last time he was with Timothy.

64 2 Timothy 1:5. Here Paul uses a word intended to counteract the character of the false teachers located in Ephesus. Paul declares that Timothy has an (ανυποκριτου πιστεως), literally translated "unhypocritical" faith, most often translated as "sincere." See Romans 12:9; 2 Corinthians 6:6; 1 Timothy 1:5; 2 Timothy 1:5; 1 Peter 1:22, and James 3:17 for this common New Testament usage of the word. Interestingly, the word "hypocrite" was the name given to Greek actors as they acted beneath a disguise. See Wuest's *Word Studies*, p. 118 for more information on this usage of the word υποκριτου. The αν placed in front of the word negates the central idea of the word, thus un-hypocritical.

65 2 Timothy 1:5. Paul's confidence in Timothy in regards to his faith was very strong. Paul wrote "I am persuaded ... " (Greek πεπεισμαι δε οτι και εν σοι). A stronger translation is supported by the use of the perfect passive form of πειθω, (1ˢᵗ person passive indicative). Literally, "I am convinced ... " See other New Testament usage of this word: Romans 8:38; 14:14; 15:14; 2 Timothy 1:12; Hebrews 6:9.

66 1 Timothy 1:18–19.

67 Based on passages like 1 Timothy 6:11 and 2 Timothy 2:16, some have suggested

deal with false teachers who questioned his teaching, and in particular, his interpretation of the Word. This, however, did not overly concern Paul, for he knew better than most the foundation upon which Timothy's life had been built. Not only had Timothy seen God work in Paul's life over and over again as he faced conflict and persecution, but his own life had been built upon the belief that the Word of God could thoroughly equip one to do God's work even against what seemed to be insurmountable odds.

The false teachers would not only attack Timothy's teaching, but his authority. In a day when the elder (πρεσβυτεροσ) was respected, Timothy was apt to find it difficult to have authority without first earning it in the eyes of the people. Paul, realizing that Timothy might be prone to react with an attack rather than acting in love, gave his young leader the following encouragement.

> *Don't let anyone look down on you because you are young, but set an example for the believers in speech, in life, in love, in faith and in purity. Until I come, devote yourself to the public reading of Scripture, to preaching and to teaching. Do not neglect your gift, which was given you through a prophetic message when the body of elders laid their hands on you. Be diligent in these matters; give yourself wholly to them, so that everyone may see your progress. Watch your life and doctrine closely. Persevere in them, because if you do, you will save both yourself and your hearers.*[68]

Timothy would need to depend on more than his character and Paul's support. He would need the constant indwelling of the Holy Spirit in order to maintain the right attitude and perspective along the way (2 Timothy 1:13–14). Without this, his ministry would be doomed.

The need for godly leadership was very clear to the apostle Paul, as time and time again he had seen those whom he had thought would be faithful

---

that Timothy was dangerously close to giving in to some of the ways of the false teachers.

68 1 Timothy 4:11–16. Paul uses the imperative form of the word καταφρονειτω, 3rd person present singular imperative of καταφρονεω; literally "to despise or scorn." Paul intended this to be an encouragement to Timothy, but also a deterrent to the Ephesian congregation and the way they viewed their young leader. The force of the word appears to be, "No one must despise your youth." Fortunately, Timothy could take certain steps toward preventing this from happening. Paul describes these later on in this particular text.

fall by the wayside (2 Timothy 2:16–18).[69] However, Timothy was different. Timothy was dependable and capable of carrying out the desires of the apostle in a way that would please God and Paul. In writing to the Corinthian believers, Paul makes clear his confidence in Timothy to get the job done.

> *Therefore I urge you to imitate me. For this reason I am sending to you Timothy, my son whom I love, who is faithful in the Lord. He will remind you of my way of life in Christ Jesus, which agrees with what I teach everywhere in every church.*[70]

Since joining Paul in his evangelistic endeavors Timothy had received an impressive education. He had heard Paul teach on countless occasions and saw that Paul's life matched what he declared from the pulpit. On a daily basis he had been a part of the unfolding commitment of Paul to bring the gospel throughout the known world, and in so doing he had witnessed a tremendous evidence of faith, patience, love, and endurance as well as persecution and suffering (2 Timothy 3:10–12).

In the mind of Paul, persecution was a way of life if one took a stand for godliness (2 Timothy 3:12). It was a time when God's servant must accept the challenge before him, unashamed and determined to allow God to work his purpose in one's life to the end (2 Timothy 1:8–12). The most important lesson of all for Timothy came not in the mere fact that there would be persecution, but rather by observing the way in which Paul dealt with persecution.

Preaching the gospel in the first century was not an easy task. Everywhere the gospel message was proclaimed, someone opposed it. At times, it was physical torment even to the point of death (2 Corinthians 11:25); while on other occasions, verbal abuse sought to destroy the character and most importantly the determination of the messenger (1 Corinthians 4:11–13).

Regardless of the form, persecution was virtually inevitable if one sought to preach a message that called men and women to repentance and challenged them to live a life worthy of the gospel. It is no wonder then that Paul admonished Timothy to "endure hardship … like a good soldier" (2 Timothy 2:3) immediately after exhorting him to pass on the truths of the faith to reliable men who could also teach others (2 Timothy 2:2).

---

69 The fact that Paul would single out Phygelus and Hermongenes suggests that Paul was particularly disturbed about their desertion, and some have argued that the language used in reference to his dear friend Onesiphorus suggests that by the time Paul had written 2 Timothy, he was dead. For more information on this thought, see: JND Kelly, p. 169ff. See also Paul's reference to the fact that Demas had deserted him (2 Timothy 4:10).

70 1 Corinthians 4:16–17.

The "passing of the baton"[71] meant that Timothy would have to work very closely with people. Unfortunately, part of the hardship in the ministry comes from the fact that people can be difficult. While the "sins of some are obvious" (1 Timothy 5:24), it is often the others whose "sins trail behind them" (1 Timothy 5:24) that create the problem in the ministry. Knowing how to deal with either type of difficult person is a challenge that must be faced.

Dealing with a difficult person in the ministry was an experience that Paul was all too familiar with and one in which he had gained some valuable insights. In order for Timothy to carry on the work started by Paul in Ephesus, he too must be able to deal with opposition that almost certainly would come his way. Fortunately for Timothy, he could be warned. Many pastors are uninformed about those people who are likely to oppose their ministry.

In Ephesus, the most visible opponent of Paul's work was Alexander. In an effort to warn and advise Timothy concerning Alexander, Paul wrote:

> *Alexander the metalworker did me a great deal of harm. The Lord will repay him for what he has done. You too should be on your guard against him, because he strongly opposed our message.*[72]

Alexander had made such an impact on his life and work that Paul was determined that Timothy knew about him and was able to cope with him, regardless of his tactics. Fortunately, Paul provided Timothy with some of the basic guidelines necessary for a leader to manage the presence of a difficult person.

Meeting Alexander[73] for the first time was probably an experience filled with anxiety for Timothy. It is one thing to meet a difficult person about whom you have had little or no prior knowledge, but it is quite another thing to meet someone about whom you have been thoroughly forewarned.

---

71 I have used the term "baton" to suggest the imagery of a race, which is consistent with Pauline theology in 1 Corinthians 9:24–27. In 1 Timothy, Paul is seen as a spiritual runner in a relay race who has reached the point of passing on the spiritual baton to the next leader. In this case, it is most definitely Timothy. Timothy would then be charged with the task of passing the baton on down the spiritual path to others who would pass it on.

72 2 Timothy 4:14–15.

73 2 Timothy 4:14. Alexander (Greek Αλεξανδρο⊠). See Bauer, p. 35, for more information. Refer to Mark 15:21; Acts 4:6; 19:33; 1 Timothy 1:20 and 2 Timothy 4:14 for a variety of biblical passages that mention the use of this proper name.

Alexander was a common name,[74] especially among the Jewish community. However, we know very little about the Alexander mentioned in 2 Timothy 4:14. Paul described him as a person who did him a great deal of harm and who strongly opposed the message (2 Timothy 4:14–15). This was not the first Alexander that Paul had difficulty with in Ephesus. In 1 Timothy Paul speaks of a man who had spoken in a blasphemous manner against the Lord (1 Timothy 1:20). Ultimately, Paul removed this man from the church in order to redeem him.[75] Although it is very tempting to identify these two Alexanders[76] as the same person, the facts are not sufficient to warrant such a dogmatic declaration. Suffice it to say that each one of these men presented a major challenge to the leadership of the Ephesian church.

The Alexander mentioned in 2 Timothy was a metal worker[77] who was

---

74 Opinions vary on the proper identification of Alexander. Some suggest that he is the Alexander of Acts 19:33, a Jew who was pushed to the forefront of a great crowd supposedly in order to voice further accusations against Paul and his companions. It is unlikely, since this happened many years prior to the experience referred to in the Pastoral letters, that this is Timothy's Alexander. Others argue that the Alexander of 2 Timothy 4 is to be equated with the Alexander of 1 Timothy 1:20. This is more likely, however it is far from being confirmed. The Alexander of 1 Timothy is one who was "handed over to Satan" in order that he, along with Hymenaeus, might learn not to blaspheme. This appears to be a temporary solution to a problem Paul was having with these men. His intention appears to be ultimately the restoration of these men to the church. If this Alexander is to be considered the Alexander of 2 Timothy, then it would appear that he had had a relapse, or was still in a state of excommunication, but nevertheless still attacking Paul and the ministry.

75 See also 1 Corinthians 5:5, 13. This action appears to be more for the purpose of redemption, then pure punishment. See also Matthew 18:17 for an explanation from Jesus about dealing with a brother who has a sin against you.

76 I prefer the idea that the Alexander in 1 Timothy and 2 Timothy are the same person. In 1 Timothy, Alexander was almost certainly excommunicated due to his opposition and statements against "sound doctrine" (1 Timothy 1:11). This, however, does not negate the possibility that Alexander was reinstated into the church and now is focusing his attack not only on the message, but is personally attacking Paul (note that he does mention the fact of a personal attack first in his final comments to Timothy in 2 Timothy 4:14–15). This fits well with the author's belief the opposition to a substantive problem, and difficulty with a person holding a different viewpoint than you, are often intermingled to the point that the difficult person sees them as one.

77 2 Timothy 4:14. (Greek χαλκεύς, nominative singular masculine, meaning coppersmith, metal worker). Kelly, on p. 217, notes that this word did not always carry with it this specialized sense and may mean here not more than a simple metal worker. Some have suggested that this Alexander was a metal worker in

able to do Paul great harm.[78] Paul's use of the aorist suggests that he most likely had a specific occasion in mind. Some have suggested that Paul is referring to an experience in Rome during his imprisonment. It has been suspected that Alexander may have appeared as a witness for the prosecution.[79] Whatever his role, it is quite certain that Alexander took an active part in opposing the work in Ephesus under the leadership of Paul. Now, at the end of Paul's ministry in Ephesus, Timothy is exhorted to be on his guard[80] against him.

In Paul's mind the church was rapidly approaching the time when the gospel would face opposition on all fronts. The last days (2 Timothy 3:1–5) are described by Paul as a time when selfishness, abuse, disobedience, unholiness, conceit, pleasure, and ungodliness would be the norm.[81] Men would become so focused on their own desires that they would literally turn away[82] from the truth and find teachers to teach their own views. It is no wonder then that Paul in his final comments to Timothy demands that he be prepared to "preach the Word; be prepared in season and out of season; correct, rebuke, and encourage—with great patience and careful instruction ..." (2 Timothy 4:2). The false teachers amongst whom we would most definitely find Alexander

the factories located in Ephesus that made silver models of the famous shrine of Artemis. Artemis was the Greek name for a goddess (Latin: Diana) who had been identified in Hellenistic syncretism with an Asiatic goddess. According to the writing of Luke in Acts 19:23ff, there was a great disturbance in Ephesus over the impact of the gospel on the work of making silver models. Paul apparently had called these models idols. Demetrius, a factory owner, was deeply disturbed and attempted to fight back against the teaching and influence of Paul. It is not certain whether the Alexander of 1 Timothy was a metal worker in the factories but it is a possibility and it would serve as a basis for much of his opposition. It is, however, definite, based on Paul's last words, that the Alexander of 2 Timothy was a metal worker (4:14–15).

78 2 Timothy 4:14. (Greek ενεδειξατο, 3rd person, singular, aorist middle indicative of ενδεικνυμαι meaning to do something with someone).

79 Kelly, p. 217.

80 2 Timothy 4:15. (Greek φυλασσου, 2nd person singular, present middle imperative of φυλασσω), meaning to guard against, look out for, avoid. A form of this word is used in 1 Timothy 6:20; 2 Timothy 1:12; 14; also see 1 John 5:21; Jude 24 and 2 Peter 3:17. Paul's purpose is that Timothy not be caught unaware of Alexander's motives and/or tactics.

81 See also Hebrews 1:2 for the idea that the "last days" began with the incarnation of Christ. Certainly, Paul's intent was to emphasize the fact that the church was going to face difficult times when people did not want to hear the sound teachings of the gospel.

82 2 Timothy 4:4. (Greek εκτραπησονται, 3rd person plural, future passive indicative of εκτρεπω), meaning to turn, turn away. See also 1 Timothy 1:6; 5:5; 6:20; and Hebrews 12:13.

were listening to hearsay and myths, yet Timothy is directed to "turn away"[83] from all that is contrary to "sound doctrine" and "guard" that which has been entrusted to his care.

> *Timothy, guard what has been entrusted to your care. Turn away from godless chatter and the opposing ideas of what is falsely called knowledge, which some have professed and in so doing have wandered from the faith. Grace be with you.*[84]

Guidelines for Dealing with Difficult People

The ministry can seem overwhelming at times. Perhaps this is the way that young Timothy felt as he heard Paul talk about the corrupt times that lay ahead, not to mention the fact that he already knew of a difficult person named Alexander who was simply waiting for him to arrive.

Thankfully, Paul not only pointed out those things that Timothy needed to be aware of, he offered sound advice about coping with the problems he might face in the ministry, even if that included a difficult person. A cursory reading of the Pastoral Epistles may not appear to offer much insight on dealing with difficult people. However, a careful study of these texts reveals a series of guidelines that a leader must follow in order to cope effectively with the presence of a difficult person.

Guideline One: Seek Balance

Following a description of what the last days will bring to the work in Ephesus, Paul states what is to be Timothy's number one priority: "Keep your head in all situations, endure hardship, do the work of an evangelist, discharge all the duties of your ministry" (2 Timothy 4:5).

There is a difference between being told to "keep your head" and "keeping your head" when it comes to dealing with conflict. The charge here is more than being calm or adhering to your principles. Paul uses a word that carries more weight and meaning than the "be sober" of the NASB[85] or the "watch thou in all things" of the KJV.[86] Here, the New International Version captures

---

83　The writer to Hebrews provides and interesting use of the Greek word εκτρεπω suggesting that a believer is called to an upright life in order that the spiritual and moral welfare of others, especially the "lame" in the Christian faith, may not waiver.

84　See 1 Timothy 6:20.

85　New American Standard Bible.

86　King James Version.

best the intent of Paul's use of the imperative νηφε,[87] which implies a freedom from confusion in the midst of conflict. Certainly this command would go well with Paul's urgent plea for Timothy to be prepared "in season and out of season" (2 Timothy 4:2).[88] He must be able to "correct, rebuke, and encourage."[89] However, it must be noticed the way in which these must be carried out in the context of ministry. Whatever approach he uses, he must never lose patience with people and must always show himself to be a source of sound judgment and a teacher of Christian truth (2 Timothy 4:2b).

The fact that Paul urges Timothy to endure hardship and to continue on in his work as an evangelist, as well as doing all of the other things that are expected of a leader, indicates that Paul did not expect or want him to stop everything in order to deal with the difficult people in the church. This, however, is exactly what some pastors do when they encounter conflict. All things come to a halt. Ministries can't continue as planned until the problem is resolved. Unfortunately, this response doesn't work in most situations and besides, this is often exactly what a difficult person desires. In essence, the difficult person has succeeded if he can cause the pastor to focus on him and stop doing the work of the ministry.

Without question this was the last thing that the apostle Paul wanted to happen to his young leader. Perhaps this is the reason that early in his second letter to Timothy Paul advises him to "fan into flame[90] the gift of God that

87 2 Timothy 4:5. (Greek νηφε), 2nd person singular, present active imperative of νηφω, meaning to be sober, well balanced, self-controlled. Kelly argues that here νηφε means more than being calm and unhurried, or even always alert, but that he should stay clear of all heretical teaching.

88 Paul uses the Greek word επιστηθι, 2nd person aorist active imperative of επιστημι meaning to stand by, be ready, be on hand. The use of two adverbs (positive and negative) ευκαιρος and ακαιρος suggests being ready, whether it seems a good time or not. Kelly notes that the imperative of command used here can have the military meaning of being "posted" or "stay at one's post." But there is no hint of this in this passage in light of the context. It would be better translated, states Kelly, as "be at one's task" and, in light of the context, this is exactly what Paul is trying to say.

89 Each of these commands uses an imperative form, indicating the importance and urgency of Paul's instructions at this point.

90 (Greek αναζωπυρειν) present active infinitive of αναζωπυρεω meaning to rekindle, kindle. This use of the infinitive suggests the idea of continual effort on the part of Timothy in the work of rekindling the flame. Some (Vincent) argue that Paul did not mean to suggest that Timothy's zeal had grown cold, yet the context would seem to suggest that something about the exercise of his faith and leadership was in need of stirring up, or bringing back to its full flame. Robertson translates this word as "keep blazing." Wuest argues that Paul

was in him through the laying on of hands" (2 Timothy 1:6). Here, Paul refers to the χαρισμα,[91] a gift that would enable him to carry out the work of the ministry. The gift is compared to a fire (cf. 1 Thessalonians. 5:19 "Do not put out the Spirit's fire … "),[92] suggesting the imagery of a flickering flame. The fact that Paul exhorts Timothy to rekindle the flame (stir it up) argues strongly for the possibility that Timothy was in need of reinforcement.[93]

The hint of anxiety that can be seen throughout the beginning of Paul's second letter presumably comes from the fact that the apostle was not only aware of Timothy's inexperience and timidity, but also due to his understanding of the major task that lay ahead of him. Because of this, Paul reminds Timothy of the divine commission given at his ordination (1 Timothy 1:18; 4:14; and 2 Timothy 1:6); of Paul's own example of suffering for the sake of the gospel; and finally, of Timothy's responsibility to carry on the "sound teaching" he had heard from his mentor to reliable men who could also teach others (2 Timothy 1:13–14; 2:12).

But how does a leader like Timothy pass on the essentials of the gospel if he is constantly being challenged by a difficult person who seems determined to undermine not only the work of the church but the pastor? According to Paul, the ability to "keep your head in all situations" begins by developing an understanding of one's perceptions against the reality of his situation.

Making a decision is a difficult task for most people, including pastors. Yet, in a real sense, our lives and even our ministries are the results of our decisions. Obviously, not all decisions impact our lives in the same way. Some affect us minimally, while others can literally change the direction of our lives. Tim Lahaye has observed that there are at least three types of decisions that we all make in our lives: **major, moderate, and minor.**[94]

---

is advocating that Timothy remember his calling and counteract what appears to be a "spirit of fear," thus, Paul states, "God did not give us a spirit of timidity, but a spirit of power, of love and self-discipline" (2 Timothy 1:7, NIV).

91   (Greek χαρισμα του θεου), translated gift of God. The same word is used by Paul in 1 Timothy 4:14, where Timothy is admonished not to neglect the gift (literally your gift, τον εν σοι χαρισματος) "which was given through a prophetic message when the body of elders laid their hands on you." See Ward, p. 77–78, for a discussion of the idea of receiving the gift through the laying on of hands. See also JND Kelly, p. 106–107.

92   1 Thessalonians 5:19. See Bauer, p. 752, for a study of quench or extinguish (Greek σβεννυτε, 2nd person plural present active imperative of σβεννυμι). Here the word is related to the subject of fire. Note the NIV's translation.

93   The argument here is not that Timothy's spiritual flame has gone out, but rather that it has burned low and is in need of constant stirring, like the embers of a fire that has lost its full flame.

94   Tim Lahaye, *Finding the Will of god in a Crazy Mixed-Up World,* (Grand

While in Ephesus, Timothy would be faced with each type of decision. On the level of a **major decision**, he would be confronted with his own willingness or lack of desire to carry out Paul's command to teach and admonish the false teachers in the Lord (1 Timothy 4:11). The degree to which Timothy was diligent in carrying out this directive would be a strong indicator of whether or not he had decided to be faithful to his commitment. In terms of **moderate level decisions,** Timothy would be challenged on a variety of issues.[95] It seems reasonable to suggest that since Timothy was young, he would make decisions that would go against the grain of thought most commonly accepted in the older Christian community. It was almost inevitable that the false teachers would take every opportunity to use this against him. It is not surprising then that Paul warns Timothy about permitting his youthfulness to be used as a mark against his leadership ability. Paul writes:

> *Don't let anyone look down on you because you are young, but set an example for the believers in speech, in life, in love, in faith and in purity. Until I come, devote yourself to the public reading of Scripture, to preaching and to teaching … be diligent in these matters; give yourself wholly to them, so that everyone may see your progress. Watch your life and doctrine closely. Persevere in them, because if you do, you will save both yourself and your hearers.[96]*

Finally, in terms of **minor decisions**, there would be many reasons for Timothy to make basic choices that would give direction to his work in

Rapids, MI: Zondervan Publishing House, 1989), p. 21. According to Lahaye, **Major decisions** have a life-directing influence on you. They include things like: salvation, vocation, marriage, education, and commitment to obedience. **Moderate decisions** influence your whole life, but they can be altered or remade more easily than major decisions. They include: where you work, where you live, where you go to church, your friends, and your children. **Minor decisions** are made many times a day. These decisions are seemingly endless and they include: which store to shop in, how to find an honest orthodontist, where to buy your next car, what kind of car to buy.

95 Timothy would be faced with a decision of what to teach and who to trust or not to trust in the church that was filled with strife.

96 1 Timothy 4:12–16, NIV. See also 2 Timothy 2:22 for another passage in which Paul admonishes Timothy to take care in the way he lives, particularly in light of the fact that he is a youth. Some have seen in this passage, as well as others in the pastoral letters, the hint that Timothy had been adversely influenced by his opposition and their tactics, as well as their beliefs. All the more reason for Timothy to be wise and make Godly decisions.

Ephesus. Decisions as simple as *What do I wear?* or as complicated as *How do I act around so and so?*, were bound to come up in the midst of Timothy's daily activity. The fact that each person and especially each leader is faced with decisions in life is clear. The need for making good decisions is also obvious. The difficulty comes in knowing how to make wise choices in the midst of so many alternatives.

Effective decision-making does not just happen. Each person (e.g., pastor) must develop a *strategy* that will enable him to make decisions that are consistent with his inner understanding of what is right. Calvin Miller calls this process "the making of pier decisions."[97] For the Christian, a pier decision is one that places God at the center of things.[98] It is a mark of spiritual maturity, notes Miller, when a leader considers how his decisions will be acceptable to God before he contemplates the benefit it will bring to him.

The ability to make decisions that are consistent with the pier decisions a person has previously made depends largely on the strategy he has chosen to use when confronted with a choice on an issue whether it be major, moderate, or minor. Many leaders struggle in their ability to make wise choices because they are predominately **reactive**, rather than **proactive**[99] in their personal strategy.

The attempt to develop a personal strategy that leads a leader to success is not new. A study on this subject by Stephen Covey, a noted researcher and teacher on the subject of personal and organizational leadership, has revealed some interesting insights. Covey identified the fact that over the past two hundred years there has been a fundamental shift in the way literature has

---

97   Calvin Miller, Leadership, (Colorado Springs, CO: NAVPRESS, 1987), p. 50–51. Miller argues that every leader needs to know how to recognize and make pier decisions.

98   Ibid., p. 50–51. For the Christian, writes Miller, "the first pier decision is to admit Christ into one's life to take His rightful place of Lordship. Evangelicals refer to this as 'making a decision for Christ.'" Yet the statement, "make a decision for Christ" is not totally honest. When you admit Christ to His rightful place of Lordship, you are really making a decision for yourself as much as for Christ. So the decision is a pier decision in every way." In essence, writes Miller, " you are deciding to bring the consultation of God into critical influence of your decision making process."

99   Larry L. McSwain and William C. Treadwell, *Conflict Ministry in the Church*, (Nashville, TN: Broadman Press, 1981), p. 38f. The authors suggest that there are two primary ways in which a person can respond when the potential for conflict is high: 1) **Reactive:** This style assumes the minister is simply to respond to whatever happens; or 2) **Proactive:** When the leader observes developing conflict, he or she acts with integrity in such a way as to influence the results of any encounter between persons.

perceived success.[100] Over the first 150 years, success was seen in terms of what he calls the **character ethic**. This paradigm[101] presented the foundation of success in terms of integrity, humility, fidelity, temperance, courage, justice, patience, industry, simplicity, modesty, and the Golden Rule. The character ethic was built on the belief that there are basic principles for effective living, and people can only experience true success and happiness as they learn to integrate these principles into their basic character.

Over against the character ethic, Covey noticed a transition in the literature of the last fifty years. Rather than an ethic that emphasized character, **personality** was now primary. Success was now being perceived as a function of personality, of attitudes and behaviors, skills and techniques that lubricate the processes of human interaction.

In an attempt to clarify the concept of a paradigm, Covey suggests that one think of a map.[102] A map is not to be confused with the actual territory, but rather an explanation of certain aspects of the territory. We all have maps in our heads that can essentially be divided into two categories: the way things are, or realities, and the way things should be, or values. In essence, a map becomes the guiding pattern for our lives. Difficulty comes when one assumes that the way he sees something is the way it really is or the way it should be.[103]

The evidence that a person is influenced by his own map is clear when it is observed that two people can see the same thing, disagree, and yet both be right. Imagine what impact a lifetime of influences (family, school, church, work, friends, etc.) can make on a person and his ability to perceive things objectively.[104] Based on personal experience, a person usually thinks that he sees things as they actually are. However, more often than not, a person sees the world and his experiences not as they are but as he is conditioned to see them.

The degree to which one is aware of his own personal map (paradigm) and the extent to which he has been influenced by them the more he can take responsibility for his actions. A person can test his map against the reality of

---

100 Stephen R. Covey, *The 7 Habits of Highly Effective People*, (New York, NY: Simon and Schuster, 1989), p. 18ff. Here Covey identifies the relationship between our inner paradigms and the values and attitudes that flow from them.

101 Ibid., p. 23. **Paradigm** was originally a Greek word that, in its original use, was a scientific term. Paradigm literally means a pattern or map for understanding and explaining certain aspects of reality. Today, it is commonly used to mean a model, theory, perception, assumption, or frame of reference. In more general terms, writes Covey, paradigm is the way we "see" the world—not in terms of our visual sense of sight, but in terms of perceiving, understanding, and interpreting.

102 Covey, p. 23.

103 Covey, p. 25.

104 See Chapter One, pages 18–25, for a discussion of the contexts of influence in a person's life.

the situation. He can listen carefully and empathetically to others and by so doing gain a better picture, an objective view.

Timothy's situation could be sensibly and effectively handled provided he was able to see the situation for what it was and remember the principles upon which he was raised. Paul, mindful of the fact that Timothy might be impressionable, and in some cases easily influenced, exhorts him to stay true to what he has learned and become convinced of throughout his life.

> *But as for you, continue in what you have learned and have become convinced of because you know those from whom you learned it, and how from infancy you have known the holy Scriptures, which are able to make you wise for salvation through faith in Christ Jesus.*[105]

However, in Timothy's situation it would appear that the giving of this command was easier than obeying it. This is not surprising given the presence of a difficult person like Alexander. Obviously, Timothy faced a challenging situation. Nevertheless, what could he do? While some leaders would suggest immediately addressing the problem situation, there are many others who believe that given this particular set of circumstances, nothing constructive could be done that would effectively deal with Alexander and the problems in Ephesus.

This approach to conflict is often based on a firm belief in the social sciences, which proposes that a person is largely determined by his conditioning or conditions in life.[106] The question is whether or not this paradigm (map) describes accurately the territory of life. Is it true that a person is a victim of his circumstances with only a few possibilities of reaction? Is it possible that in any given situation a person is only capable of responding like a Pavlovian dog in the experiment of life? Does this perception agree with reality?

One might speculate what would happen if young Timothy had taken this kind of view toward the task of staying in Ephesus in order to deal with false teachers. From the outset Timothy knew about the presence of people who had

---

105 2 Timothy 3:14–15, NIV.

106 Covey, p. 67–68. There are three social maps—three theories of determinism widely accepted, independently or in combination, to explain the nature of man. *Genetic determinism* basically says that your grandparents did it to you. It just goes through the generations, and you inherited it. *Psychic determinism* basically says your parents did it to you. Your upbringing, your childhood experiences essentially laid out your personal tendencies and your character structure. *Environmental determinism* basically says your boss is doing it to you, or your spouse, or that bratty teenager, or your economic situation, or national policies. Someone or something in your environment is responsible for your situation.

abandoned their faith (1 Timothy 1:19–20) and were living as if they had no conscience (1 Timothy 4:2). The church was filled with tension, as the women and men were apparently disputing over their proper roles both in and out of the church (1 Timothy 2:8–15). The ministry in Ephesus was burdened by people who sought the pleasure of money and false teachings to the point that they had not only brought many difficulties into their own lives, but ruined the faith of others (1 Timothy 6:3–10). People in Ephesus were also involved in godless chatter that, if allowed to go unchecked, would only get worse (2 Timothy 2:16 –18). If that weren't enough, there was one man who was most likely going to be Timothy's faithful foe, Alexander (2 Timothy 4:14–15).

It is quite apparent that this was not the most appealing ministry situation. Given the condition of the church and the fact that these beliefs, attitudes, and practices were present, is it unrealistic to think that Timothy might assume that there was no chance of resolving the problems. Most definitely if he merely reacted to the circumstances.

Human beings, however, are not just feelings, moods, or even thoughts. The fact that a person can think separates him from all other creations. He can see himself, check his paradigms, and determine whether they are reality based or simply a result of his conditions. The question is, Why did Timothy not give in or give up in light of what clearly appears to be incredible odds? The answer lies in the problem.

Timothy was determined that he could make a difference in the midst of a bad situation, and he believed that he could deal with Alexander. Why? The reason is plain. For many people, the way they see the problem *is the problem*. This, however, was not true for Timothy, as he had the freedom to choose to do something different. He was not restricted by his environment or the troubling situation in Ephesus. This is not to say that he was not influenced by the external stimuli, whether it was social, physical, or psychological. But, rather, that at the center of his life there was a reason to believe that he could make a difference for the good.

Christ-Centered Principles

Timothy's confidence[107] came not from the fact that he was significant or possessed some special power, but because he was "n Christ" and it is "in Christ" that Timothy knew all things could be done (Philippians 4:13). Like

---

107 It is interesting to note that this is exactly what Timothy had to be reminded of in the second letter of Timothy. Paul was confident of Timothy's sincere faith, therefore he reminded him of the fact that God had not given him "a spirit of timidity, but a spirit of power, of love, and of self-discipline" (2 Timothy 1:7).

Paul, for Timothy being "in Christ" was the most succinct description of the believer's relationship to Christ.[108]

> *Therefore, if anyone is in Christ, he is a new creation; the old has gone, the new has come. All this is from God (2 Corinthians 5:17–18, NIV).*

In the words of Philip Hughes, this is one of the most concise and profound statements in all of scripture, declaring the "inexhaustible significance of man's redemption."[109] Hughes more graphically states:

> *It speaks of security in Him who has Himself borne in His own body the judgment of God against our sin; it speaks of acceptance in Him with whom alone God is well pleased; it speaks of assurance for the future in Him who is the Resurrection and the life; it speaks of the inheritance of glory in Him who, as the only-begotten Son, is the sole heir of God; it speaks of participation in the divine nature in Him who is the everlasting Word; it speaks of knowing the truth and being free in that truth in Him who Himself is the Truth. All this, and very much more that can be expressed in human language, is meant by being "in Christ." No wonder that the Apostle describes it in absolute terms as the "new creation."Redemption in eternal purposes in creation, so radical in its effects that it is justly called a new creation.[110]*

The new creation Paul speaks of represents the beginning of a new life. It is a life motivated by the love of Christ which was demonstrated through his sacrifice for all.

> *For Christ's love compels us, because we are convinced that one died for all, and therefore all died.[111]*

---

108 (Greek εν Χριστω Iησου), translated "in Christ Jesus." This is a common phrase in the pastorals (as well as other Pauline epistles) indicating Paul's emphasis upon the fact that the believer's life is centered or anchored "in Christ." See 2 Timothy 1:1, 9, 13; 2:1, 10; 3:12, 15.

109 Philip Hughes, *The New Testament International Commentary on the New Testament: I Corinthians* (Grand Rapids, MI: William B. Eerdman's Publishing Co., 1962), p. 201.

110 Hughes, p. 202.

111 2 Corinthians 5:14–15, NIV.

The true believer no longer lives for himself. Now, Christ is the operative presence and power in his life. The transfer of commitment away from self/sin and toward Christ is the result of what Paul could have called *the death of "I"*:

> *I have been crucified with Christ and I no longer live, but Christ lives in me. The life I live in the body, I live by faith in the Son of God, who loved me and gave himself for Me.*[112]

The new life that is created "in Christ" is a glaring contradiction to the practice of those in the world. While the committed believer centers his life in Christ, it is not uncommon for others to build their lives on things other than Christ. Yet, according to Paul, to have anything but Christ at the center of your life can only lead to ruin. Because Timothy had Christ at the center of his life, he was able to cope with the situation at hand. Because of Christ, he was a **principle-centered leader**. His principles came from the Word of God, which is capable of thoroughly equipping the man of God for "every good work" (2 Timothy 3:17).

The inner strength that gave Timothy the initiative to accept the responsibility of staying in Ephesus in order to deal with a troubled church is likewise available for today's leader through the experience of a "paradigm shift"[113] in his thinking. No longer can a leader of today rely on the power of his own personality, or even in his character to see him through. He must rely on the competency of Christ (εν Ξριστω).[114] Through a renewal of his commitment to be "in Christ" and a faithful determination to be obedient to God's Word, a leader can confidently face the task of working with a difficult

---

112 Galatians 2:20, NIV. Here Paul uses the phrase "I have been crucified with Christ" (Greek χριστω συνεσταυρωμαι). See F.F. Bruce, *New International Greek Commentary: Galatians,* (Grand Rapids, MI: William B. Eerdman's Publishing Co., 1982), p. 144 for his discussion on the relevance of using the perfect tense. Bruce suggests that in using the perfect tense Paul wanted to emphasize that participation "in Christ" has become the believer's settled way of life. Note: While the Galatians text is a figurative death, see the gospels (Mt. 27:44; Mark 15:43; John 19:32) for texts about the two thieves who died "with Christ" (Greek συσταυρωθεντες συν). The difference between these men and believers is that Christ died in our place. To put it another way, we were "with him" on his cross.

113 **Principle-centered leadership** is a term I have borrowed from Covey and applied to the Christian leader. Christ is the center of the believer's life, and the principles are based upon the Word of Christ (The Scriptures). See footnote number 49 for an explanation of the author's use of paradigm.

114 (εν χριστω) means "in Christ." This is a common phrase used by Paul to speak of the believer's close relationship with Christ.

person. This, however, is only the beginning of the journey for the leader who wants to cope effectively with his difficult person.

Perceptions: Distiguishing the Problem from the Person

A major part of the pastor's effort to bring resolution to a problem situation hinges on his ability to distinguish the problem from the person.[115] This is extremely important when one considers that in many cases the way a person sees a problem *is* the problem. A person's perception of a problem can be greatly affected by their own emotions, values, background, and viewpoints. Therefore, any attempt to resolve a problem will be significantly enhanced by making every effort to distinguish between the issue and the person. In addition, a leader's own understanding of his personal makeup can affect the potential resolution of a problem.[116]

Christian leaders and especially pastors not only need a keen awareness and understanding of their own personalities and behavioral tendencies, but a sufficient grounding and understanding in the biblical principles that apply to the task of dealing with difficult people. Otherwise, a leader's own personal pattern of behavior might override God's plan of intervention. In a case like this, a leader may be prone to react according to his preferences rather than respond to the specifics of a given need in a Christ-like manner. Leaders who understand their personality, behavioral patterns, and have a grasp of God's principles for dealing with people possess not only the initiative, but the **"response-ability"** to make things happen that are consistent with their beliefs. This type of leader does not easily fall prey to blaming the circumstances or conditioning for his behavior. On the contrary, his behavior

---

115 Robert Fisher and William Ury, *Getting To Yes: Negotiating Agreement Without Giving In*, (New York, NY: Penguin Books, 1982), p. 18. The authors suggest that a major consequence of the "people problem" in negotiation is that the parties' relationship tends to become entangled with their discussions of substance. The various people problems related to substantive issues write Fisher and Ury fall into one of the three categories: 1) Perception; 2) Emotion; 3) Communication. See this text for a helpful discussion on these categories, p. 17–39.

116 Francis Littauer, *Personality Plus: How to Understand Others by Understanding Yourself*, (Tarrytown, NY: Fleming H. Revell Company, 1983), pp. 7–17. In this book, Littauer provides the results of her latest study in the field of personality development. It is her most recent attempt to show how your unique blend of traits can affect your emotions, work performance, and relationships. Perhaps the best contribution in this book is the **Personality Profile Test,** which can be easily taken, scored, and interpreted. Littauer argues that by understanding your own temperament, one can be freed to act in a way that is consistent with who you are and not in accordance with someone else's strategy.

is a direct result of a conscious choice, based on solid principles from the Word of God and a balanced view of human behavior.

Christian leaders who possess these qualities are potentially very effective in the pastoral ministry. The fact that he has made a pier decision[117] to follow Christ gives direction and stability in his life and ministry. Choosing to follow Christ not only provides an anchor in the leader's life, it also enables the leader to serve others. Jesus himself said:

> *Love the Lord your God with all your heart, and with all your soul and with all your strength and with all your mind; and love your neighbor as yourself.*[118]

The leader's ability to obey the second command is contingent upon obeying the first.

The Need for Patience

Serving other people is not intrinsic in our nature. For this reason, we must first come to the Lord. By coming to Christ with our hearts, souls, minds, and strengths, we receive the substantive power to love others. Our model for loving others can be clearly seen in the way that Christ loved us. Paul was keenly aware of the depth of God's love for him (1 Timothy 1:12–14). He also understood that God wanted this kind of love to be seen in his life (1 Timothy 1:15–16).

This principle equally applies to the task of seeking to understand another person. By taking a close and honest look at one's own personal attitudes and behavior against the backdrop of God's love and compassion, a leader can begin to grasp and accept the attitudes and behavior of another person. This insight can be of particular interest and assistance when a leader is asked to cope with a difficult person.[119]

---

117 The Christian's initial pier decision is to commit their lives to Christ (traditionally called making a decision for Christ) and to obey his commands. By nature of this decision, all other lifestyles, philosophies, etc., are considered unacceptable. God's Word becomes the "plumbline" for all future decisions.

118 Luke 10:27, NIV.

119 McSwain and Treadwell, p. 170–183. These authors have identified the fact that most people tend to respond to all conflict similarly. This is called their **primary style of ministry**. If the primary style of conflict ministry does not work, then they will go to another approach. Among their list you will find: 1) The Problem Solver, 2) The Super Helper, 3) The Power Broker, 4) The Facilitator, 5) The Fearful Loser. Also included in this fine book is a list of resources for dealing with one's personal assessment of conflict management. See page 184ff for information on the **Change Agent Questionnaire** by Jay

The process of loving God first and then others was a key factor in Timothy's effort to "keep his head in all situations." He not only had to challenge his perceptions with the reality of the situation, he needed to exercise patience in the midst of what was most likely a very challenging situation. Being patient is especially helpful for the leader as he seeks to gain a clear comprehension of the problem.

Patience Builds Perspective

Long before a pastor can begin to intervene effectively into a conflict situation, he will need to know the exact nature of the problem. Determining the real problem is not always a simple task, and failure to identify the real problem at times becomes the key obstacle in moving a problem situation toward a satisfactory resolution.

Although a difficult person may give many reasons for a leader to be suspect of his behavior and words, intentionally reading certain meanings into his actions can only confuse the issue. Unfortunately, however, quick and unfounded judgments abound in the church today, and it would be unwise to minimize their impact on the church.[120] Yet how many times have we heard one member judging another before knowing all of the facts? How many friendships have struggled to survive the thoughts of suspicion without seeking to know the truth? How many churches have been torn apart due to a quick and hasty judgment based on hearsay or only half of the story? How many pastors have been tried, judged, and hung because people have made up their minds before

Hall and Martha Williams. This tool is designed to measure one's philosophy, strategy, and evaluation of effecting change. Also check out the work by Jay Hall entitled **Conflict Management Survey**. This tool helps the leader determine his own conflict management style by responding to a variety of conflict situations. See James Hinkle and Tim Woodruff, *Among Friends*, (Colorado Springs, CO: NAVPRESS, 1989), p. 209–217. These authors do an excellent job of addressing the subject of conflict management. They are referenced at this point because they present in their material a copy of Norman Shawchuck's **Conflict Style's Inventory**. This inventory is simple and easily scored. It has been said that management is doing things right, while leadership is doing the right things. The **Management Traits Analysis** is a helpful survey that classifies management into four categories: The Promotional Manager, The Concept Manager, The Operational Manager, and The Negotiating Manager. This survey is taken from Myron Rush's work entitled *Managing To Be The Best*, (Wheaton, IL: Victor Books, 1989).

120 Horace L. Fenton, Jr., *When Christians Clash*, (Downer's Grove, IL: Intervarsity Press, 1987), p. 42–48. Fenton shares some valuable insights on how to avoid "jumping the gun on judgments" (i.e., learn the difference between judging and discernment).

hearing the whole story? Any pastor can give testimony to the fact that many heartaches have been caused by people who have been quick to judge.

The arch enemy of quick judgments and the key tool for counteracting hasty conclusions for the leader is discernment. It is an indispensable tool given by God through a faithful study of His Word (2 Timothy 3:15–17). For young Timothy, discernment would be one of his most valuable assets in fighting the opponents of "sound doctrine" (1 Timothy 1:10).[121] The last days (2 Timothy 3:15), according to Paul, would be a time when discernment and a careful diagnosis of the behavior and the teaching of the day would be absolutely essential.[122] Timothy was charged with the task of bringing the teachings of the Word to those who tended to gravitate to teachings and behaviors that are contrary to the pattern of life that "conforms to the glorious gospel of the blessed God … " (1 Timothy 1:11).

Timothy was to be ready in season and out of season to correct, rebuke, and encourage with great patience and careful instruction (2 Timothy 4:2). The command to exercise patience for Timothy was based on Paul's own testimony of the purpose of God's patience in his life.

> *Here is a trustworthy saying[123] that deserves full acceptance. Christ Jesus came into the world to save sinners—of whom I am the worst. But for that very reason I was shown mercy so that in me, the worst of sinners, Christ Jesus might display his unlimited patience as an example for those who would believe on him and receive eternal life.[124]*

121 See also 2 Timothy 4:3; Titus 1:9, 2:1 for other pastoral passages using the phrase "sound doctrine."

122 Philip Babcock Cove (ed.), *Webster's Third New International Dictionary*, (Springfield, MA: G. & C. Merriam Company:, 1966), p. 644. This English word is taken from the Latin *discernere,* meaning to separate and distinguish between. This can be broken down even further in meaning. *Discernere* is taken from *dis* (apart) and *cernere* (to sift). Definitions range from: 1) to detect or discover with other senses than vision; 2) the inductive apprehension of a truth imperfectly; 3) the ability to analyze the essentials of complicated questions. Diagnosis (p. 622) means to determine the cause of or the nature of a problem by virtue of discernment. I have chosen to use these two words because they best describe the task that lay before Timothy as he dealt with the false teachers and their teaching.

123 1 Timothy 1:15. (Greek πⲭστος ο λογος), meaning "faithful the Word." See other sayings like this, which are used in the Pastoral Epistles (1 Timothy 3:1; 4:9; 2 Timothy 2:11; Titus 3:8). These are perceived by many as key sayings to Timothy in the Pastoral Epistles.

124 1 Timothy 1:15–16, NIV.

Paul's hope and prayer was that Timothy, along with everyone else, might see in him evidence of the impact of God's patience, and that somehow this testimony would further the work of the gospel. Paul knew better than any the significant role God's patience had played in his coming to Christ. Because of this, he emphasized the importance to Timothy of exercising patience when dealing with difficult people.

When attempting to work effectively with difficult people, patience is an absolute necessity,[125] especially since it is through the exercise of patience that the potential and hopefully eventual transformation of the difficult person is made possible.[126] By practicing patience, a pastor invites God to bring about the resolution of a conflict prior to using him as an instrument of change. However, should God choose to use the pastor, by being patient he is given the chance to study God's Word from a nonjudgmental and non-confrontational point of view in order that he might be able to intervene at the appropriate time and in an appropriate manner.

The modern-day pastor[127] faces a tremendous challenge when one

---

125 Note: I did not say efficiently but effectively. Trying to work efficiently puts a leader on a time table that might not work given the particular dynamics of a situation. It is particularly frustrating if efficiency is the goal to discover that a difficult person has a different plan (and they usually do) and goal.

126 2 Timothy 2:25–26, NIV.

127 By the use of this term, I am referring generally to the pastor of the last thirty years. Specifically, I have in mind the pastor that has been influenced by a culture that places a high degree of importance on producing results quickly. The emphasis upon "instant" results has affected much of our society, even the church. It is also my conviction that this type of cultural mindset has adversely affected the pastor and the way his role is perceived today. The pastor himself has even come to see himself as the "spiritual fix-it" person in the congregation, which results in a ministry largely absent of patience. Ironically, there is present today a thought that perceives the pastor as one who has no self-esteem, despite the "fix-it" mentality, and is seeking to develop it by professionalizing the ministry. For a consideration of this line of thinking, see: Os Guiness and John Seel, (eds.), *No God, but God: Breaking with the Idols of our Age*, (Chicago, IL: Moody Press, 1992) chapter nine entitled "The D.-MIN.-IZATION of the Ministry" (p. 175–188). In this chapter, David F. Wells writes that the pastorate is losing credibility due to the way it is trying to gain it. Also, see David Gadoury, "Developing and Measuring Pastoral Competency: A Resource for Non-Traditional Theological Education," 1984), p. 89–99. In this unpublished doctoral thesis written at Gordon-Conwell Theological Seminary in South Hamilton, MA, Gadoury, along with a committee, identify a list of 204 ways in which a pastor needs to be competent. Fortunately, Gadoury and the committee categorize this list into a workable small list of seven (teach, preach, administrate, counsel, worship leader, equipper, and shepherd). This is an extensive list of responsibilities and

considers all of the demands and expectations that are placed upon him as he attempts to carry out what might be considered the primary tasks of the pastor-leader. Timothy was exhorted by Paul to be devoted, diligent and to persevere in such ministry activities[128] as the public reading of the Word,[129] and the preaching[130] and teaching[131] of the Word. In addition, he was to make

---

sheds some valuable insights into the problem facing the pastorate. Could it be that the ministry has become so broad in the eyes of the pastor and the people that the real work of the ministry cannot be adequately carried out?

128 Some have suggested that the practice of these ministries were intended to provide us a model as pastors. See Gordon Fee, *New International Biblical Commentary: 1 & 2 Timothy, Titus*, (Peabody, MA: Hendrickson Publishers, 1984), p. 107 for the suggestion that although this certainly refers to what Timothy is to do in public worship, it is too narrow a view to see this as intending to provide a model. We know that public worship included prayers (2:17; 1 Corinthians 11:2–16), singing (Colossians 3:16; 1 Corinthians 14:26; cf 1 Timothy 3:16), charismatic utterances (1 Thessalonians 5:19–22; 1 Corinthians 11:2–16; chapters 12–14), and the Lord's supper (1 Corinthians 11:17–34). It seems more likely that these are to be viewed as Timothy's primary way of countering the false teachers in the church (2 Timothy 3:14–17).

129 (Greek τηαναγνωσει) translated "public reading of the scripture." See Luke 4:16; Acts 13:15; 2 Corinthians 3:14. Perhaps even Colossians 4:16; 1 Thessalonians 5:27; Revelation 1:3 for the reading of additional portions of the New Testament. Most likely this is a reference to the reading of the Old Testament passages predominately with a focus more on what is read rather than how it is read. However, for a recent consideration of the work of reading the scriptures publicly see: Thomas Edward McComiskey, *Reading Scripture in Public: A Guide for Preacher and Lay Readers*, (Grand Rapids, MI: Baker Book House, 1991).

130 (Greek τηπαρακλησει) meaning "preaching and taken from the word παρακλησις. This word is used extensively by Paul. Παρακαλεω (comfort) is found 103 times in the N.T., 54 times in Paul. Παρακλησιςis found 29 times in the N.T., and 20 times in Paul. John and James do not use the words. In 2 Corinthians 1:3, Paul calls God the God of comfort and in Romans 15:4, he writes of the way the scriptures are an encouragement (Greek παρακλησεως). In Acts 13:15, a sermon that Paul is about to give in Psidian Antioch is called a message of encouragement (NIV, Greek παρακλησεως). Note especially in 2 Corinthians 1:3–4 that by retaining comfort for both the noun and the verb, we get the full force of the original. For this thought see: Ralph Earle, *Word Meanings in the New Testament*, (Grand Rapids, MI: Baker Book House, 1974), p. 247. The same comfort we receive from God is invited to overflow to others.

131 (Greek τη διδασκαλια) meaning "the teaching." The previous task and this one are combined in 1 Timothy 6:2b, and is translated "these are the things you are to teach and urge on them" (NIV). Timothy is to give his time and effort to teaching against the ετεροδιδασκαλειν (see 1 Timothy 1:3) of the false

every effort not to neglect his spiritual gift[132] (1 Timothy 4:13–14), which would enable him to carry out these responsibilities.

The task of preaching and teaching would be especially challenging for Timothy in view of the fact that Paul expected him to "gently instruct" (2 Timothy 2:25, NIV) those who opposed him with the hope that many would turn to the truth. In Paul's life and ministry, opposition was not uncommon and had come in a variety of ways. Nevertheless, he was intent on not allowing opposition to thwart the advancement of the gospel (2 Corinthians 6:3–10). Through the exercise of patience, the gospel was presented and Paul was able to experience the power of God's grace upon his life and ministry (2 Corinthians 6:1).

In the mind of Paul, it was patience that would permit the leader to unlock the door leading to understanding in the midst of conflict.[133] Attempting to unlock the door with haste would be seen by Paul as counterproductive.[134] The tendency for leaders to act in haste is often brought on by the belief that one's neglect to intervene immediately can only make the conflict worse. However, according to the words of David, it is the act of patiently waiting before the Lord that actually makes the promise and experience of peace possible.

> *Be still before the Lord and wait patiently for him; do not*
> *fret when men succeed in their ways; when they carry on their*

teachers who do not agree with the sound instruction of the Lord Jesus Christ (1 Timothy 6:3). Elsewhere in the Pastoral Epistles, this participial form of the verb used in 1 Timothy 1:10 (Greek υγιανουση) from which we get hygienic is translated sound. Here it is rendered as wholesome. Apart from the three times in the Pastorals, and three times in Luke, this word is only found in 3 John 2. Some have used this to suggest that Luke may have had a considerable part in the writing of the Pastoral Letters.

132 (Greek του εν σοι χαρισματος) translated "the in you gift." In Paul's writings, there appears to be a close connection between gift and Spirit. See 1 Corinthians 1:7; 12:4, 31; Romans 1:11. The word is often translated as "spiritual gift." In this sense, the gift most certainly pertains to the calling and gift for ministry as a preacher and teacher of the Word. It is through the exercise of this gift that Timothy is to overcome the influence of error (cf. 1 Timothy 1:13–14; 2:15; 2:24–26; 3:14; 4:5). Timothy must rely on the Holy Spirit (see 2 Timothy 1:6–7, 14) who is the source of the gift he is not to neglect (Greek μη αμελει, 1 Timothy 4:14) translated "disregard" or "not take care of."

133 Perhaps Paul was reminded of the proverb that reads, "A patient man has great understanding, but a quick-tempered man displays folly" (Proverbs 14:29, NIV).

134 See Proverbs 19:2: "It is not good to have zeal without knowledge, nor to be hasty and miss the way" (NIV).

wicked schemes. Refrain from anger and turn from wrath; do not fret—it leads only to evil. But the meek will inherit the land and enjoy great peace.[135]

In order to fulfill this command, Timothy and every leader must walk down a path that is prepared by the Lord. The writer of the Proverbs puts it this way:

> *Trust in the Lord with all your heart and lean not on your own understanding; in all your ways acknowledge him, and he will make your paths straight.*[136]

Trusting God completely in the midst of conflict is never easy. In reality, few leaders are equipped to complete this task. However, by walking obediently along this path, the Christ- centered leader can learn to face the challenges of life in the pastoral ministry and be able to join with the apostle Paul in declaring that one has "fought the good fight ... " (2 Timothy 4:7).

Many valuable lessons can be learned along this path that will enable the leader to cope with any problem[137] he might face in the ministry. It is along this path that Timothy was able to position himself for an effective ministry, one that focused on being right with God first, then others (1 Timothy 4:7–8).

The first step along this path is one of **preparation** (2 Timothy 4:2). In order to cope with difficulty in the church, the leader must be prepared. This was a primary focus of Paul's closing comments to Timothy (2 Timothy 4:1–2). During this time of preparation, the leader is given an opportunity to examine himself in order to make sure that he is in the faith. Paul's closing words to the believers in Corinth reveal this practice.

---

135 Psalm 37:7–8, 11 (NIV). See also Proverbs 15:18 and 19:11. The focus of this Psalm in its first two sections (1–7) and (8–11) is to call on individual members of the community of people to trust in Yahweh alone, even in the face of powerful opponents and oppressors. The point is not to become upset with injustice (v. 1, 7, 8) but to trust and delight in God alone (v. 3, 5) and to wait on Him (v. 7). Ultimately, God's righteousness will prevail (v. 2, 9, 10).

136 Proverbs 3:5–6, NIV. See also Proverbs 11:5: "The righteousness of the blameless makes a straight way for them, but the wicked are brought down by their own wickedness."

137 Paul wanted Timothy to be prepared for every situation because he knew that conflict could arise anytime. Sometimes conflict arises when you least expect it. See Dobson, Leas, and Shelly, p. 109–118 for a discussion of what they call the ten most predictable times of conflict in the church.

Examine yourselves to see whether you are in the faith; test yourselves. Do you not realize that Christ Jesus is in you, unless, of course, you fail the test?[138]

By walking along this path of preparation, the leader can make sure that he is living the faith "in Christ" versus in the power of the flesh. Any man-made strategy is just that, man-made, if only used in the power of the flesh.[139] Therefore, every leader must be certain that he is living "in Christ" before confronting difficulty of any kind.

The next step along the leader's path is one of **submission** (2 Timothy 1:12). Living one's life according to the flesh is a lifestyle of self-gratification. Paul describes this life as being in conflict with life by the Spirit (Galatians 5:17). In Galatians Paul addresses the subject of freedom in Christ, which is a freedom to serve others (Galatians 1:4) rather than a freedom for self-indulgence (Galatians 5:13). Once again, Paul describes the walk of faith "in Christ" as a journey of **submission**, both to Christ and to others.

You my brothers were called to be free. But do not use your freedom to indulge the sinful nature; rather, serve one another in love. The entire law is summed up in a single command: "Love your neighbor as yourself."[140]

Living "in Christ" is a life of commitment to the one who is able to work in and through us despite our insufficiencies.[141] Having believed in Christ and crucified our sinful nature along with its desires on the cross of Christ (Galatians 5:24), the Christian leader is to be completely submitted to Christ and put his "hope in the living God, who is the Savior of all men, and especially of those who believe" (1 Timothy 4:10, MV). Paul knew that the work of submitting ourselves fully to Christ and to others would not easy. Realizing that it was easier to train ourselves for an immediate physical

---

138 2 Corinthians 13:5, NIV.

139 See 2 Corinthians 5:16–17, literally "according to the flesh" (Greek κατα σαρκα). Notice Paul's emphasis upon being "in Christ" (Greek εν Χριστω) and the fact that this is the foundation upon which our new lives are built. All the old ways of looking at things; life and people changed when we became centered "in Christ" (vs. 17). The result of being "in Christ" is that we now become ambassadors of reconciliation for Christ urging men and women to come to Him in faith too.

140 Galatians 5:13–15, NIV.

141 2 Timothy 1:12.

reward, Paul admonished Timothy to train himself to be spiritually godly, for it had eternal value both for now and in the life to come (1 Timothy 4:7–8).

Spiritual maturity can be seen in the life of a leader when he is able to submit to another person in the midst of conflict rather than fighting for his so-called rights.[142] Sometimes, submission can lead to a period of waiting on the Lord to reveal His will for one's life.

The next step along the path that leads to intervening effectively in a difficult situation is the development and practice of **patience** (2 Timothy 4:2; Greek μακροθυμια). The exercise of patience does not prohibit the accomplishment of God's will. Being patient does not mean to do nothing until God does something. Patience means to work hard doing God's will for your life in your context of ministry. Patience means letting God work in the hearts and minds of men and women while you are carrying out all the duties of your ministry (2 Timothy 4:5).

Learning to exercise patience comes from exercising patience. In this experience of waiting on the Lord, we realize like the psalmist of old that the Lord will answer. David wrote: "I waited patiently for the Lord; he turned to me and heard my cry ... " (Psalm 40:1).

The continuation of this Psalm in verses 24 points out the next step that a leader must take as he walks along the path. It is a step that often leads to **sacrifice**.

> *David declared: He lifted me out of the slimy pit, out of the mud and mire; he set my feet on a rock and gave me a firm place to stand. He put a new song in my mouth, a hymn of praise to our God. Many will see and fear and put their trust in the Lord.*[143]

142 Just a quick reminder of Paul's teaching on the matter of rights in the life of the Christian. See 1 Corinthians 9:15 where Paul, despite the fact that he had rights based on his accomplishments, chose not to use any of them so that he might not discredit the gospel. More importantly, he did it so that he might save some. Paul wrote, "I have become all things to all men so that by all possible means I might save some. I do all this for the sake of the gospel, that I may share in its blessings." Without submission to God's will and a denial of his own, Paul would not have been able to do these things in his ministry.

143 Psalm 40:24. Note that it is after David had trusted God through this experience that God answered and used this as a testimony to those around him of God's faithfulness and love. This is noticeably similar to Paul's understanding of how God works when he admonishes Timothy to be patient so that God could use the example as a testimony to those who would believe on His name (1 Timothy 2:16).

The walk of faith and submission by a leader in the presence of a difficult person can often lead to the need for sacrifice. A difficult person can, and in many cases, will bring much pain, heartache, and agony into the life of a leader. Nevertheless, one's willingness as a leader to stand with Christ daily and rely on his strength (Philippians 4:13), despite the consequences, promises to lead to a life filled with great reward both for now and in the future (2 Timothy 2:12).

Finally, it is a path along which a leader can learn God's **principles** (2 Timothy 2:15, 3:16). David wrote that God had "laid down precepts that are to be fully obeyed" (Psalm 119:4, NIV). These precepts (principles) are discovered and understood only if God reveals them. David longed for this spiritual illumination of God's Word so that he might live in accordance with them. He writes:

> *I am your servant; give me discernment that I may understand your statues.*[144]

And

> *Open my eyes that I may see wonderful things in your law.*[145]

David truly saw God's words as the instrument of victory against his enemies. He believed that by finding and understanding God's principles and being diligent in keeping them, he could do the Lord's will.

> *Oh, how I love your law! I meditate on it all day long. Your commands make me wiser than my enemies, for they are forever with me. I have more insight than all my teachers, for I meditate on your statues. I have more understanding than the elders, for I obey your precepts. I have kept my feet from every evil path so that I might obey your word. I have not departed from your laws, for you yourself have taught me. How sweet are your words to my taste, sweeter than honey to my mouth! I gain understanding from your precepts; therefore I hate every wrong path. Your word is a lamp to my feet and a light for my path.*[146]

---

144 Psalm 119:125, NIV.
145 Psalm 119:18, NIV.
146 Psalm 119: 97–105, NIV.

Paul also knew that it was not enough simply to know and understand God's principles. Therefore, he admonished young Timothy to do his very best[147] to obey the principles of the Word every day and in every way. A leader's commitment to this task will not only bring approval by God, but enable him to work with even the most difficult person (2 Timothy 3:16; 4:12).

Guideline Two: Seek God in Prayer

Guideline One involves the **preparation of the leader**. **Guideline Two** draws the leader and God together in agreement on the process of how to bring healing into a problem situation. If conflict is going to be dealt with in a way that is pleasing with God, leaders must not only **"keep their head in all situations"** in order to prepare themselves for the conflict; **leaders must pray**.

Therefore, it is to the subject of **prayer** that I now turn your attention. By understanding the general purpose of prayer in the Bible and its specific role in regards to dealing with a difficult person, a leader is one step closer to making a positive difference for the cause of Christ in the church when conflict arises. With this hope in mind, it is in the spirit of the words according to the psalmist that we pray.

> *I call on you, O God, for you will answer me; give ear to me and hear my prayer. Show the wonder of your great love, you who save by your right hand those who take refuge in you from their foes.*[148]

---

147 (Greek σπουδασον) meaning "be diligent" or "do your very best." See 2 Timothy 2:15. Here, Paul reminds Timothy that winning an argument is not enough. Besides, for the Christian leader, engaging in an argument is unacceptable. A Christ-centered leader must not only know God's truth, but do his very best to live it out in his life ("correctly handle the word of truth.") as well as apply it to the lives of others.

148 Psalm 17:6–7, NIV.

Chapter Three
Conflict and Prayer

The pages of the Bible are filled with testimonies to the fact that conflict is a reality of life. The scripture is also clear on how one should respond in the midst of conflict. The words of the Lord Jesus are especially meaningful for the Christian concerning this subject. On many occasions Christ spoke of the need for patience, understanding, and ministry to be given to those who opposed one's thinking and behavior. In Matthew's gospel we read the words of Jesus, which are intended to serve as a basic principle of response for the Christian as he encounters conflict with another person.

> *You have heard that it was said, 'Love your neighbor and hate your enemy.' But I tell you, Love your enemies and pray for those who persecute you, that you may be sons of your Father in heaven ....*[149]

This gospel account reveals the Lord's desire for the believer when he is confronted with a situation of conflict that includes a difficult person. First, the Christian is to love his enemy. Second, he is to *pray* for the person who opposes him no matter what the offense. Loving and praying for one's enemies makes it possible for the believer to please the Father in heaven (vs. 45), and to become more like the Father (vs. 48) over against the practices of the pagans (vs. 47).

The desire to love and pray for an enemy can only come by accepting

---

149 Matthew 5:43–45a, NIV.

and experiencing God's kind of love, not man's.[150] Through experiencing God's love, one can be moved beyond a superficial level of caring for another person and brought face to face with God's demand for Christians to love everyone, even their enemies. God's love sets a high standard and has many characteristics,[151] yet perhaps none captures the heartbeat of his love more than the quality of forgiveness. In view of God's love and forgiveness, it is not surprising that the apostle John declared, "This is love: not that we loved God, but that he loved us and sent his Son as an atoning sacrifice for our sins."[152] Experiencing God's love through the acceptance of his forgiveness makes possible the beginning of a life of love for the believer (1 John 4:11).[153] It is not a love based on merit, but a love grounded in the compassion of God, given even while we were lost and unwilling to come to Him.[154]

A person's response to God's love and forgiveness can lead him to act in one of two ways. He can respond negatively, like the king's servant of old (Matthew 18:21–35) [155] who thought that only he deserved forgiveness, and reap the undesirable results of having an unforgiving spirit (Matthew 18:32-35) or he can respond positively. Responding positively to God's love and

---

150 (Greek αγαπατε) 2ⁿᵈ person plural active imperative of αγαπατω, to love (Mt. 5:44). This Greek word as suggested by W.E. Vine, *An Expository Dictionary of New Testament Words*, (Old Tappan, NJ: Fleming H. Revell, Co. 1952), Vol. 3, Lo-Ser, p. 20–21 is a powerful word that speaks of God's love toward us and our love for others. Here Vine describes this word as "the characteristic word of Christianity." This type of Christian love, whether expressed toward specific people or toward men/women in general, is not an impulse from the feelings; it does not always run with the natural inclinations, nor does it spend itself only upon those for whom some affinity is discovered. This agape love seeks the welfare of all (see Romans 15:2).

151 See 1 Corinthians 13:18a, NIV.

152 1 John 4:10, NIV.

153 The following verse (1 John 4:12) indicates that the best way to experience a confirmation of God's love in our own lives is to begin to love others. Yet the ability to love others begins with the fact that God has first loved us (1 John 4:10).

154 See Romans 5:8 for the teaching that "while we were still sinners, Christ died for us" (NIV). This is the same kind of love that God wants us to practice in regards to those who sin against us. See passages like Matthew 6:12; 14–15; Matthew 18:21, 35; Luke 11:4; etc., for the importance of and the role of forgiveness.

155 A parable told by Christ to his disciples in order to teach the meaning of forgiveness and the importance of practicing forgiveness with others in accordance with the forgiving spirit of the Lord.

forgiveness is not without its blessings,[156] but, more importantly, it makes possible the blessing of others through a life that has been changed.[157]

The difficulty in responding positively to conflict is that as people we have limits while God does not. However, forgiveness and love are exactly what God expects of a believer when he finds himself in a conflict with a difficult person. Like Peter, many people would prefer drawing a definitive line over which a difficult person cannot cross.[158] Jesus, however, argues quite strongly for an attitude of patience when it comes to the offensive talk and behavior of another person. In fact, according to Jesus, the potential for a person to experience love and forgiveness lays squarely on the spiritual shoulders of every believer (John 20:21–23, NIV):

> *Peace be with you! As the Father has sent me, I am sending you. And with that he breathed on them and said, receive the Holy Spirit. If you forgive anyone his sins, they are forgiven; if you do not forgive them, they are not forgiven.*

The believer is not only required to love his enemies; he is expected to forgive them. According to Jesus, to pray effectively for a difficult person in a conflict situation, that person must be forgiven, and if necessary the leader should reconcile himself to that person in advance of coming to the throne of God (Matthew 5:23–24). This understanding of the believer's responsibility when dealing with interpersonal conflict is reinforced by the Lord's model

---

156 See Luke 6:37–38 for the context of this statement by the Lord. Each admonition in this text is put in the negative (i.e., do not judge) in order to show that the result of obedience in each area will be positive (i.e., you will not be judged). Jesus' phrase, " will be measured to you … " is repeated by Paul in Galatians 6:7, when he states, "a man reaps what he sows."

157 See Paul's words in 2 Corinthians 5:16–19. In this passage, Paul emphasizes the role of the believers as they carry out God's plan of ministry. No longer are we to look at people through the eyes of flesh, but rather through the lens of the cross. Due to Christ's death on the cross, we are forgiven of our sins, and Christ is now carrying his message into the world through us ("We are Christ's ambassadors, as though God was making his appeal through us" vs. 20, NIV).

158 See Matthew 18:21. The account of the unmerciful servant in 18:23–35 begins with Peter coming to Christ and asking him about putting limits on forgiving a brother who has offended him or, as Peter put it, "sins against me?" Jesus did not accept Peter's attempt to quantify forgiveness. The fact that Jesus says "seventy times seven … " (490 times) was not intended to mean for Peter to count to 490 times and then stop forgiving. Jesus' intent seemed to be that Peter should not be worried about how many times he had to forgive another person, but rather that he be busy forgiving people.

prayer in Matthew 6:9–13,[159] which teaches that before our debts[160] can be forgiven, we must forgive the sins of those for whom we are praying.

Forgiving the sins of our enemies is a difficult task, especially if their sins have been directed at our lives and ministries. However, repulsive as this may sound, it is precisely the task given to each of us by the Lord Jesus Christ. He first mentioned it to his disciples during a time when he was seeking to prepare each of them for the opposition that they would experience in living out the principles of the kingdom (Luke 6:22, NIV) against those who Jesus called enemies—those who hate you, curse you, and mistreat you (Luke 6:27–28). Over against what might be a more human response, Jesus called upon his disciples to love, bless, and more importantly pray for them.

Praying When You Would Rather Not

— *The Example of James*

When faced with a difficult decision, praying is not always a person's first response, yet it is the biblical response. This is especially true when the situation is filled with conflict. The apostle James advised the recipients of his letter with these words of instruction when they were faced with a problem: "Is anyone of you in trouble, he should pray?"[161] This passage is significant for the development of a biblical understanding of the role of prayer in conflict. The message of this particular passage is especially relevant and must be understood within the context of James' entire book, which is addressed to a

---

159 See Matthew 6:12, NIV. (Greek αφηκαμεν) 1st person plural aorist of αφιημι, meaning to forgive. This particular word emphasizes the fact that the prayer is offered by one who has already forgiven the person for whom they are praying. This is significantly different than a prayer that is dependent of whether the pray-er forgives someone or not. Mark 11:24–25 indicates that an unwillingness to forgive another person can block the effectiveness of a person's prayer. For a further discussion of this matter, see: William David Spencer and Aida Besancon Spencer, *The Prayer Life of Jesus: Shout, Revelation of Love, a Commentary*, (Lanham, MD: University Press of America, Inc., 1990), p. 28ff.

160 In the Matthew account, the Greek word οφειληματα, accusative plural nominative of οφειλημα, ατος, το, meaning debt, what is owed, one's due, debt or sin; direct object of αφες. In the Lukan account (11:24) the Greek word αμαρτιας is used. In the second part of verse 4, the Greek, literally says "everyone who is indebted to us." The Greek word is οφειλοντι, dative singular masculine present active participle of οφειλοω, meaning to owe, be indebted. In the Lukan account, the word for sins and debts are used interchangeably which leads to a similar understanding in both passages.

161 James 5:13, NIV.

group of believers who were becoming frustrated with the demands of living for Christ in the midst of persecution.

The advice given by James to his readers, namely to persevere (James 1:14) rather than fighting or running from persecution, is based on the realization that in persecution God often does his greatest work in our lives. James understood that fleeing from a problem will never accomplish God's righteousness in the life of the believer (James 1:19–20), therefore he admonishes Christians to respond appropriately when faced with a trial.

The apostle was writing to a group of people who were struggling with inconsistency in their faith. This was described by James as ακαταστατος (Greek for uncontrollable, unstable), a condition that was clearly illustrated in their talk (James 3:10).[162] The most discouraging thing for James was the fact that the members of the church had begun to eliminate God from their world view. Rather than coming to the Lord, they busily pursued their own remedies to life's problems. James makes it clear in his letter that this is not God's desire. For James, God is a God for those who are in need, not for those who need nothing.

The plea of the book of James is not restricted to praying. On the contrary, James exhorts believers to express their contentment and confidence in God through a variety of expressions such as joy, singing, confessing, or praying (James 5:13–16). He begins his discourse in this particular passage by asking a series of questions. Each question is intended to cut to the heart of the believers walk with the Lord. James' first question and the question of interest for us at this point is one of experience. He asks, "Is any one of you in trouble? He should pray." Here, James uses a word (Greek κακοπαθει), meaning to suffer hardship.[163] The force of the indicative is helpful in understanding the intent of James. He is not so concerned about the past troubles in the lives of the believers, but rather with those they are presently experiencing.[164] *The Everyday Bible*[165] captures the flavor of this request by stating, "If one of you is having troubles …." Through his words we catch the urgency of James' exhortation. This is not something that the believer should put off doing, but rather he should pray now.

---

162 "Out of the same mouth come praise and cursing. My brothers, this should not be." (NIV)

163 James 5:13. 3rd person singular present active indicative of the Greek word κακοπαθεω.

164 This is a helpful and interesting thought, especially when one remembers the importance of loving and forgiving your difficult person, which I've already discussed. James is interested in dealing with the problem at hand. This should also be the major concern of every leader.

165 Thomas Nelson, *The Everyday Bible: The New Century Version of the Bible*, (Dallas, TX: Word Books, Inc., 1987).

In this instance James uses a form of the familiar word προσευχομαι.[166] While the indicative indicates that the action is taking place in the present, the middle voice represents the subject as participating in the results of the action, as having a personal interest in the labor. To James, the most important thing a believer can do in the midst of persecution is pray, and the benefits both for the recipient of the prayer and the one who prays are significant.

The apostle James is quite familiar with the troubles that one can experience in the walk of faith (James 1:2, 12). He is keenly aware of the part that suffering plays in developing us into mature believers (James 1:4). Like James, Paul too writes about the significance of suffering hardship in the ministry. His personal "gospel" was filled with suffering (2 Timothy 2:9); therefore, it is not surprising when Paul admonishes Timothy to endure hardship as a vital part of his ministry (2 Timothy 4:5).

Unfortunately, it is not uncommon for believers to get discouraged as they cope with their troubles. Therefore, James reminds them of Job (James 5:10–11). By recalling the experience of this Old Testament patriarch, the believers are reminded of a classic example from the history of God's people when God honored the faithful prayers of a servant. In the face of suffering (κακοπαθειας, James 5:10),[167] Job persevered and God heard his prayer. According to James, each believer should follow Job's example by praying immediately and continuously in their own time of trouble. The resulting answer may be immediate, or it may come later (James 5:7–11). Regardless, the believer should pray.

Their prayers, according to James, must be prayers of faith (James 5:15 –16). To drive home his point, James refers to another Old Testament prophet (Elijah) to emphasize the effectiveness of a prayer given in faith. Elijah was a human being just like each of us (Gk.ομοιοπαθης),[168] which must mean that he was susceptible to times of trouble, rejoicing, and sickness. James' point is clear and equally relevant for us today. If God would answer the prayers of a righteous man named Elijah in a time of need, who was just like us, he will certainly answer the prayers of a righteous[169] man or woman today. In fact, argues James, this kind of prayer is tremendously effective.[170]

---

166 προσευχεσθω, 3rd person singular present middle imperative of προσευχομαι, meaning to pray.

167 Genitive singular feminine of κακοπαθεια, ας, η, meaning suffering, misfortune, and misery.

168 James 5:17. Greek ομοιοπαθης, nominative, singular, masculine, adjective of ομοιοπαθης, ες, with the same nature.

169 Greek δικαιου, meaning righteous one, James 5:16.

170 James 5:16. Greek ενεργουμενη, nominative singular feminine present middle participle of ενεργεω, meaning to work or be effective.

Efficient or Effective Praying?

– *A Prayer Meeting in Ephesus*

Most leaders yearn for a prayer life that is filled with power, yet at the same time are quite emphatic that prayer should be the centerpiece of their ministries. Nevertheless, experience would indicate that emphasis alone is insufficient in meeting the ongoing needs that arise in the daily work of the leader. The answer to the demanding needs and problems faced in the life of the church is not necessarily more prayer. It is no longer adequate simply to think of prayer in terms of earnestness.[171] More than ever, lay people and especially leaders are discovering the need for prayers that are effective.[172]

Without question, according to 1 and 2 Timothy, the ministry in Ephesus had reached a level of need where prayer was not an option, but a necessity. In fact, Paul writes early on in his first letter about the importance of Timothy praying for everyone:

> *I urge, then, first of all, that requests, prayers, intercession and thanksgiving be made for everyone—for kings and all those in authority, that we may live peaceful and quiet lives in all godliness and holiness. This is good and pleases God our Savior, who wants all men to be saved and come to a knowledge of the truth.*[173]

Timothy more than likely had little trouble being obedient to this task, particularly since he had made the acquaintance of Alexander the metalworker (1 Timothy 1:20; 2 Timothy 4:14–15). According to Paul's second letter,

---

171 I have used this term in order to emphasize the idea of those who think that the most important thing in prayer is to be serious and diligent.

172 Building on the term used by the apostle James in 5:13–18 (Greek ενεργουμενη) nominative singular feminine present middle participle of ενεργεω, which means to work or be effective, James combines this word with another one that means to have power, be competent or be able (Greek ισχυει) 3rd person singular present active indicative of ισχυω. These two words together suggest that James has in mind a prayer that not only gets the job done, but does so with power.

173 1 Timothy 2:13, NIV. This passage sets the tone for the entire book in terms of how Paul expects Timothy to go about dealing with the problems in Ephesus. This is significant when one considers how often leaders are guilty of jumping right into the problem without spending time with the Lord in prayer.

Alexander had been determined to make Paul's life and ministry miserable and from all indications was now transferring his activity to Timothy.

The pattern for Timothy's prayer life was clear in Paul's mind. His prayers were to include everyone, and he was to pray in a variety of ways.[174] Through his prayer life, Timothy would enable[175] God to work in the ministry and in the lives of people in such a way as to cause them to do their work well and in so doing maintain a social and spiritual climate that was conducive to carrying on the effective work of the church and its gospel.

There were many issues in the ministry at Ephesus. These issues were important to Paul and Timothy. They were important for the simple fact that if allowed to go unchallenged, they would not only cause people to "shipwreck" (1 Timothy 1:19) their faith, but the entire future ministry of the church would be in jeopardy. Some of the issues that Timothy faced were the distortion of the law (1 Timothy 1:6–10); the relationships and roles of men and women in the home as well as in the ministry (1 Timothy 2:8–15); the influence of deceptive spirits in following false doctrines (1 Timothy 4:1–5); the care of widows and the future of young widows in the church (1 Timothy 5:3–16); the lack of proper respect for the leaders in the church (1 Timothy 5:17–20); the allegiance of some people to the false security that was thought

---

174 In this passage (1 Timothy 2:13), Paul describes a variety of prayers that are referred to in the Bible. First, he uses the word requests (Greek δεησεις), which means entreaty or requests. This makes sense in that God is the one who can hear our questions. He not only can hear them, but he can do something about them. Paul exhorts Timothy to make all of his requests to the Lord (see Isaiah 59:12; Jeremiah 29:12–13). Paul's next word is a common word for prayer (Greek προσευχας). The fact that the other words used in this text seek to capture the wide array of prayers in the New Testament apparently caused Paul to list this one in order to make sure that all approaches to the throne of God are utilized. Thirdly, Paul uses the Greek word εντευξεις, accusative plural feminine of εντευχις, εως, η, meaning petition or intercession. Certainly, this emphasizes the fact that Timothy needed to bring before the Lord exactly what he wanted him to do and be faithful in bringing it before him. Finally, the word thanksgiving (Greek ευχαριστιας) accusative plural feminine of ευχαριστια is used to suggest the idea of thanksgiving in the prayer life of Timothy. Timothy would encounter many problems in Ephesus, and being thankful would pay great dividends in Timothy's life and ministry, especially when he faced Alexander. These types of prayer together argue for a comprehensive approach by Timothy as he comes to the throne of God in order that God might work in Ephesus in a mighty way and that the gospel might go forward.

175 The use of this word is not meant to suggest that God is incapable of working without our prayers. But, rather, that Timothy is inviting God to work and is willing to get out of the way or be obedient in any way that God might seem fit in order to bring about his will in a particular situation.

to be found in the things of this world (i.e., money, 1 Timothy 6:3–10); the task of remaining pure, holy, and righteous in the midst of a pagan society (2 Timothy 2:20–22); the responsibility of ministering to those who opposed the gospel in a gentle but firm fashion (2 Timothy 2:23–26); the work of keeping true to the Word of God, despite having to face persecution (2 Timothy 3:10–17); the preaching of the Word faithfully even when people choose to pursue the thinking and ways of the world (2 Timothy 4:1–5); and finally, the challenge of facing a difficult person like Alexander who has already made known his opposition to the things of God, as well as the servants of God (2 Timothy 4:14–15).

Any leader would consider these kinds of problems as major obstacles in one's ability to carry out the work of the ministry. Instinct suggests that the most effective way to deal with this kind of situation is to get busy working on the problems. This, however, in many ways goes against the advice being given by Paul to Timothy. Paul expected Timothy to pray and allow God the opportunity to work on the problem. This attitude toward problems, which is proposed in the Pastoral Epistles, can also be seen in the words and experience of David, (See Psalm 27:1–6, 13–14 and Psalm 40:1–2). It can be clearly seen in these two Old Testament passages that David believed and practiced waiting on the Lord and that the Lord was more than faithful in responding to the need. In fact, David writes about the difference God made in the situation after he willingly and prayerfully waited on the Lord by saying, "He put a new song in my mouth, a hymn of praise to our God" (Psalm 40:3a). This advice is echoed in Paul's letter to the Roman believers when he wrote, "be joyful in hope, patient in affliction, faithful in prayer."[176]

What, however, could be expected for Timothy as a result of his faithfulness in prayer? What significant difference would it make if Timothy prayed for the problems in Ephesus? Is it reasonable to believe that God cared about Alexander to the degree that the prayers of Timothy for this difficult person could actually open the door to an effective way of ministering to him? Apparently, this is exactly what Paul had in mind as he gave these instructions to his young apostolic delegate. After a further look at Paul's communication to Timothy, one is able to discern a variety of interesting and noteworthy insights regarding the inner workings and dynamics of praying for a problem and in particular, another person.

Prayers that Make a Difference

Years ago the psalmist David wrote the following words because he believed that his prayers would make a difference. He was convinced of the loving

---

176 Romans 12:12, NIV.

character of his God and certain that He would act on his behalf in a way that would meet his every need.

> *Hear, O Lord, and answer me, for I am poor and needy. Guard my life, for I am devoted to you. You are my God; save your servant who trusts in you. Have mercy on me, O Lord, for I call to you all day long. Bring joy to your servant, for to you, O Lord, I lift up my soul. You are forgiving and good, O Lord abounding in love to all who call to you. Hear my prayer, O Lord; listen to my cry for mercy. In the day of my trouble I will call to you for you will answer me.*[177]

The fact that Timothy's greatest concern in Ephesus was a person like Alexander did not change the fact that prayer was to be his highest priority. The goal of prayer in his mind, as well as in the mind of Paul, was that prayer would pave the way for a peaceful and quiet coexistence with Alexander (1 Timothy 2:2) as well as provide direction in regard to a host of other problems. The question for Timothy and for every leader who faces a difficult person in his place of ministry is simple: "How will prayer make a difference?" It is not until chapter four of Paul's first letter to Timothy that we find part of the answer to this most important question.

> *for everything God created is good, and nothing is to be rejected if it is received with thanksgiving, because it is consecrated by the word of God and prayer.*[178]

This verse is potentially troubling to a leader if the phrase "everything God created is good ... " (1 Timothy 4:4) is to be taken to include difficult people. One's natural tendency is to avoid trouble and focus on those things that are considered to be worthy and manageable. However, it would appear that Paul included Alexander in "everything" and did not exclude him by using the term "nothing." In the book of James we read similar advice when

---

177 Psalm 86:1–7, NIV. This passage presents many common aspects of our discussion to this point: a) David calls to God because of his need and when he is in trouble (v. 1, 7); b) David is devoted to his Lord because he knows that God is loving and caring and will do what is best for him (v. 5); c) David calls on his Lord constantly, for he is devoted to him and he trusts him (v. 2); d) David expects his Lord to bring him mercy and joy, even in the midst of his predicament (v. 3, 4, 6). David believed that his God answers him. Therefore, he called on him (v. 7).

178 1 Timothy 4:4–5, NIV.

the apostle declares that opposition comes in the form of various kinds of trials.

> *Consider it pure joy, my brothers, whenever you face trials of many kinds, because you know that the testing of your faith develops perseverance.*[179]

Indeed, Timothy's faith would be tested in Ephesus through a variety of pressures. According to this text, Timothy would be faced by those who made it their business to tell other people what they should do and should not do. For Paul, it was clearly a sign of the times when people would "abandon the faith and follow deceiving spirits and things taught by demons" (1 Timothy 4:1). He made it clear that these kinds of teachings come from "hypocritical[180] liars, whose consciences have been seared as with a hot iron" (1 Timothy 4:2). Who better to pray for them than a young leader, despite his weaknesses, that contrary to his opponents had been described as one with an "unhypocritical faith"[181] (2 Timothy 1:5)?

The imagery of having your "conscience seared as with a hot iron"[182] (1 Timothy 4:2) is significant when one thinks about the importance of being able to discern what is right from what is wrong. Having lost all sensitivity to spiritual things, it was now up to Timothy to minister to these people in such a way that would reach them with the gospel. The people who opposed Timothy and the ministry in Ephesus were not interested in what was right. In fact, they were unable to determine that on their own. They were concerned about promoting a way of thinking that fit into their man-made philosophies

---

179 James 1:2–3, NIV.

180 (Greek υποκρισει) dative. Singular feminine of υποκρισις, εως, η, meaning hypocrisy and pretense. With εν, it is translated "in hypocrisy." Note the comparison to Timothy who had an "un-hypocritical" faith (2 Timothy 1:5).

181 (Greek ανυποκριτου) genitive singular feminine adjective of ανυποκριτος, ον, meaning genuine, sincere modifying faith. Literally translated as "un-hypocritical."

182 (Greek κεκαυστηριασμενων) genitive plural masculine perfect passive participle of καυστηριαζω, meaning to brand with a hot iron or sear. Paul describes the false teachers as having had their consciences "seared or cauterized" as with a hot iron. The passive is used by Paul in order to emphasize the fact that the false teachers were the ones receiving the action of the verb. In this case, the false teachers were having their consciences seared. See 1 Timothy 1:5 and 3:9 for the fact that this was in opposition to the Christian person who had a good or clear conscience. See also Ephesians 4:19, where Paul uses a similar term to convey the losing of one's moral sensitivity (Greek απηληκοτες) nominative plural masculine perfect active participle of απαλγεω.

and theologies. In the mind of Paul, the task that faced young Timothy included teaching these people what was right and acceptable in the sight of God.

> *If you point these things out to the brothers, you will be a good minister of Christ Jesus, brought up in the truths of the faith and of the good teaching that you have followed .... Be diligent in these matters; give yourself wholly to them ... persevere in them, because if you do, you will save both yourself and your hearers.*[183]

The idea of confronting a difficult person with the error of his ways is not a pleasant thought for any leader. Yet how many leaders have prematurely confronted a person only to discover that they had made a mistake in judgment? In most situations of conflict, some kind of confrontation is virtually inevitable yet not always immediately necessary. The significant point being made by Paul is the fact that Timothy can choose his confrontational experience through a study of the Word[184] and time spent in prayer. Long before Timothy would get the chance to "gently instruct" Alexander (2 Timothy 2:25), he would reflect at great length on the biblical principles that had guided him throughout life and spend much concentrated time in prayer on his behalf.[185] According to Paul, the burden of accepting this task lay solely on the shoulder of those "who believe and know the truth ..." (1 Timothy 4:3 NIV). This, of course, included Timothy.

---

183 1 Timothy 4:6, 15, 16, NIV.

184 Refer to 2 Timothy 3:16 for a closer look at the potential role of the Word of God, particularly its ability to be used as a tool of rebuke and correcting. See also chapter 2, page 76ff, for a brief discussion on the importance of Timothy depending on the Word of God for guidance.

185 See Charles E. Hummel, *Tyranny of the Urgent*, (Downers Grove, IL: InterVarsity Press, 1967), p. 13. In this little but extremely insightful booklet, Hummel speaks of the role of prayer in the life of Jesus. He writes, "Very early in the morning, while it was still dark, Jesus got up, left the house and went off to a solitary place where he prayed" (Mark 1:25, NIV). Here is the secret of Jesus' life and work for God: *He prayerfully waited for his Father's instructions and for the strength to follow them.* Jesus had no divinely drawn blueprint; he discerned the Father's will day by day in a life of prayer. By this means, he warded off the urgent and accomplished the important.

The Specific Role of Prayer

Praying in the midst of conflict is not abnormal. Most if not all leaders have spent varying degrees of time praying when faced with a difficult decision, especially if that decision involves what to do with a difficult person. The questions that face us now and perhaps those which were on the mind of young Timothy many years ago include: (1) how are we to pray for a difficult person and (2) what could conceivably be expected from a leader's time spent in prayer on behalf of his opposition? Interestingly, part of the answer to these questions can be found by taking a closer look at the word **sanctify,**[186] which Paul uses to describe the result of turning to the Word of God and prayer when confronted by a difficult person and his ways.

From this passage of scripture, we receive a remarkable picture of Paul's thinking as it pertains to sanctifying something or someone. Generally speaking, to sanctify something is to set it aside for a special purpose.[187] This concept of what it means to sanctify something can be clearly seen in the book of Exodus, where the Lord sanctifies those parts of the ram that belong to Aaron and his sons.[188] Later in the same text, the Lord sanctifies the "tent of meeting and the altar … " as well as Aaron and his sons to serve him as priests.[189] This view of sanctify suggests that by setting apart something that is not holy to be used for bringing glory to God, that "something" is made holy.

This understanding of sanctify can also be seen in regards to people. In 1 Corinthians 7, Paul speaks of the way in which the decision of an unbelieving husband or wife to stay with his believing husband/wife sanctifies both the husband/wife and the children (1 Corinthians 7:12–16). According to the apostle's thinking, the most likely way for an unbelieving partner to be "saved" is to be in the arena of influence provided by the presence of the believing mate. On the other hand, there is little and in some cases virtually no chance of the unbelieving partner being "saved" if the believing partner leaves and removes his/her godly influence. Therefore, Paul instructs those

---

186 1 Timothy 4:5 (Greek αγιαζεται) 3rd person singular present passive indicative of αγιαζω, to make holy, sanctify.

187 There are a number of verses in the New Testament that shed light on the proper understanding of what it means to "sanctify" something or someone. See Matthew 23:19; John 17:17–19; 1 Corinthians 6:11; 1 Corinthians 7:14; Ephesians 5:26; 2 Timothy 2:21; Hebrews 9:13–14; Hebrews 13:12. The 2 Timothy and John passages are especially interesting in that Timothy and Jesus took the first step to "sanctify" themselves before being able to assist in the future sanctification of someone else.

188 See Exodus 29:27.

189 See Exodus 29:44.

believing partners to stay if they have the opportunity to do so because they do not know whether or not their mate will be saved by their presence.

This brings us to the most significant aspect of this text. Paul's closing questions, "How do you know, wife, whether you will save your husband? Or, how do you know, husband, whether you will save your wife?"[190] suggest the possibility that the unbelieving mate might be saved if the believing mate remains a vital part of the relationship. Determining exactly what Paul means by the word "save" is our next task, but prior to that it must be noted that based on this verse one can also see that the Old Testament practice of setting apart something that is not holy in order to use it to bring glory to God also applies to people. By keeping someone who is not holy in a close relationship with someone who is already being "sanctified," the potential for that someone becoming holy is enhanced.

This biblical principle of "sanctifying" something or someone is used in 1 Timothy 4:15 by Paul to show the potentially positive effect of prayer on a problem or person when he/she/it is brought before a holy God. By praying for a difficult person such as Alexander, Timothy was placing him within God's arena of influence and enabling God to bring about His will in the situation. Like the unbelieving husband in 1 Corinthians, Alexander was now in a position to be influenced or "saved" as he was allowed to come in contact with a holy God without the premature intervention of a leader.

The word "saved" as used by the apostle in this passage is difficult to understand when trying to grasp Paul's intended meaning. Obviously, Paul chose a common New Testament word that can have a variety of meanings.[191] A closer look at Paul's use of this word in other key passages helps us to develop a better understanding of Paul's teaching. The New Testament uses three words to speak of the idea of being saved,[192] with each providing a different shade of meaning. Of the ninety-two times that the New Testament uses these words, forty-five times these words carry the idea of making or keeping something/someone sound or safe.[193] There is certainly no passage in all of the Pauline literature that has caused more theological debate than the passage found in 1 Timothy 2:8–15. In this text Paul uses the word ⬚⬚⬚⬚ to describe the eventual reward of women[194] who continue in "faith, love, and holiness with propriety ... " (1 Timothy 2:15, NIV).

---

190 1 Corinthians 7:16, NIV.

191 1 Corinthians 7:16. (Greek σωσεις) 2nd person singular future active indicative of σωζω, meaning to save rescue or deliver.

192 (Greek σωζω, διασωζω, σωτηρια) See 2 Timothy 2:15; Acts 27:43; and Luke 1:71 respectively for examples of the use of each word.

193 Robert L. Young, *Analytical Concordance to the Bible*, (Grand Rapids, MI: William B. Eerdmans Publishing Company, 1978), p. 838.

194 1 Timothy 2:15. Literally σωθησεται, which is translated "she will be saved"

Much debate has taken place over the point Paul is making to Timothy regarding the role of women in Ephesus. Most of the discussion revolves around a proper understanding of the way in which Paul uses the idea of being saved. Although there is a difference of opinion regarding this verse and its intended meaning, there is general agreement that Paul is not talking of salvation in the sense of being saved from one's sins. This is supported by Paul's additional declaration that women will be saved if "they continue in faith, love and holiness with propriety" (1 Timothy 2:15, NIV).

The key to unlock this verse's meaning is considered by many[195] to be the words found in Genesis 3:16, "I will greatly increase your pains in childbirth; with pain you will give birth to children." According to the context, it would appear that the women in Ephesus were acting outside of their God-given roles (certainly their cultural roles), which was causing great turmoil within the Christian community. Paul's words in 1 Timothy 2:15 are intended to give direction to the women in the community as to how they could renew a right relationship with man and God. It is suggested by scholars like Kelly that if women stay within the boundaries of their God-given role (motherhood in this instance), rather than seeking to usurp their masculine counterparts (largely due to the influence of false teachers), they will obtain salvation. In practical terms this meant that the women of Ephesus could be put into a position where they would not lose the relationships they had with their husbands and the eternal relationship that was possible with God if they would stay within certain God-given boundaries.

Given this understanding of the usage of the word σωζω[196] in 1 Corinthians and 1 Timothy, along with a clear grasp of what it means to be sanctified, one can better determine what Paul's intentions were in 1 Timothy 4:1–5 when he

---

not women.

195 See J.N.D. Kelly, p. 69–70 for one scholar who believes in the importance of this verse for understanding Paul's teaching in 1 Timothy 2:15.

196 See Gordon Fee, *New International Bible Commentary: 1 and 2 Timothy, Titus,* (Peabody, MA: Hendrickson Publishers, 1984), p. 74–76 for a further look at the available options of interpretation. Fee suggests a variety of ways in which the word σωζω has been interpreted in 1 Timothy 2:15: (1) "will be kept safe through childbirth … "; (2) they will be saved from the errors in verses 11–12; (3) through childbearing should be translated through *the* childbirth; that is, through Mary's giving birth to Jesus. Fee notes that Paul more likely intended that woman's salvation from the transgressions brought about by similar deception (to that of Eve) and ultimately for eternal life, is to be found in her being a model, godly woman, known for her good works (v. 10; df. 5:11). He suggests that the reason for Paul to say that *she will be saved* is that it follows directly out of his having said "it was the woman who was deceived and became a sinner … " (1 Timothy 2:14b).

declares that "everything God created is good and nothing is to be rejected if it is received with thanksgiving, because it is consecrated (sanctified) by the word of God and prayer." It would be very tempting for young Timothy to run (even literally) from his problems in Ephesus, particularly his problem with Alexander, but God had given him a powerful tool by which he could counteract the work of evil with the influence of the holy. By sacrificing his own desires and committing to the way of the Lord, Timothy was now in a position whereby he could let go of Alexander and watch God work in ways that he could never have imagined. Through a prayerful surrender (an act of sanctification) of Alexander to God, Timothy would be able to "let go" of him and allow him to be placed in an environment of influence, a place where God could work on his heart and possibly bring him to a point of repentance (2 Timothy 2:25–26).

The Work of Prayer

Praying over a difficult situation or for a difficult person is demanding work for the leader, yet it is the most effective way for him to enable God to become intimately involved in his daily experiences. These daily experiences often serve as a spiritual magnet for the leader, drawing him into a time of concentrated prayer. This was the experience of Moses many years ago. Fresh off the experience of dealing with Miriam and Aaron's opposition (Numbers 12:1–16), the people of Israel were planning to move on in their journey, thus Moses gave the order to go and check out the land (Numbers 13:17–20). The order was carried out until the scouts returned and a conflict arose among the people of Israel about whether they should go and take the land.

It is possible that Moses, the scouts, and the people could have come to an agreement on what to do had it not been for the fact that some of the dissenters decided to spread their message of doom among the people of Israel (Numbers 13:31–33). Although Caleb and Joshua supported the plan to go and take the land, the people refused to listen to their advice. The "daily experience" in the life of the people of Israel escalated to the point that there was even talk of stoning the leaders. Fortunately, God intervened.

God's intentions were clear. He was going to destroy those who opposed his plans to move the people of God into the land of promise. Knowing God's plan, Moses began to pray. Like Abraham of old, Moses prayed to God and interceded on behalf of his people, even the dissenters. Moses wanted God to carry out his will, but he earnestly prayed God would do something other than destroy the people of Israel (Numbers 14:15–19). As a result of prayer, God honored Moses' request. He still accomplished his will, but he rewarded the faithful petitions of Moses, who prayed for his people.

Moses was drawn to prayer because he knew that it was in prayer that God's power was made available to his people. Paul also knew this truth, which is the reason he did not procrastinate in telling his young apostolic delegate to pray for everything and everyone (1 Timothy 2:14). The urgency and the importance of this exhortation by Paul can be seen in the use of the word παρακαλω.[197] Here, the idea is about one who is being exhorted to ready himself for a spiritual battle to be fought out on the fields of a leader's prayer life.

The spiritual leader who fails to heed the warning calls of a potential battle and neglects whatever preparation is necessary to fight must also be willing to experience the negative results of a life without prayer. In his book *Too Busy Not to Pray*, Bill Hybels provides a clear and candid description of the potential results for a leader who neglects turning to God in a time of need.

> *The other side of that equation is sobering: it is hard for God to release his power in your life when you put your hands in your pockets and say, 'I can handle it on my own.' If you do that, don't be surprised if one day you get the nagging feeling that the tide of battle has shifted against you and that you're fairly powerless to do anything about it.*

> *Prayerless people cut themselves off from God's prevailing power, and the frequent result is the familiar feeling of being overwhelmed, overrun, beaten down, pushed around, and defeated. Surprising numbers of people are willing to settle for lives like that. Don't be one of them. Nobody has to live like that. Prayer is the key to unlocking God's prevailing power in your life.[198]*

Attempting to handle problems in the ministry by yourself, especially those involving difficult people, can result in what Roy Oswald calls the "deadly cycle"

---

197 Paul uses a present active indicative of παρακαλεω (1 Timothy 2:1), meaning to exhort, admonish, or encourage. See Fritz Reinecker, *A Linguistic Key to the Greek New Testament* Vol. 2: Romans-Revelation, (Grand Rapids, MI: Zondervan Publishing House, 1980), p. 29, for the idea that this word was used in classical Greek of exhorting troops who were about to go into battle. Here it is a request based on the apostolic authority of Paul. See also Romans 12:1.

198 Bill Hybels, *Too Busy Not to Pray: Slowing Down to be with God* (Downers Grove, IL: InterVarsity Press, 1988), p. 11. Bill Hybels is the leader of Willow Creek Community Church in the Chicago, IL area.

that begins with the high ideals of one's commitment to ministry, cycles through the pressures of more human need than can be met, and results in physical exhaustion and strain on family and other relationships. The minister feels hopeless and trapped and resents parishioners, church, and the whole situation. Feeling guilty for all these reactions, the minister rededicates to trying even harder, and the cycle goes around again.[199]

A leader can avoid this "deadly cycle" by participating in what Ralph Herring calls a "Cycle of Life"[200] that promises to bring hope and encouragement into a difficult situation or relationship. At the heart of this "cycle" is prayer, prayer that places the leader in a close relationship with the God of all creation and all knowledge. Rightly so, Herring raises the question as to why prayer should take precedence over any other means by which we as believers receive from God's hand of grace. Based on a study of Romans 11,[201] Herring discovers and shares that even prayer flows in a cycle to God and becomes the most effective means for a leader to tap into God's redemptive plan.

It is God's triumph of spiritual engineering, employing all his gifts and providing unlimited access to all the resources of his being. Prayer is a summit meeting in the very throne room of the universe. There is no higher level. As all lines within the pyramid converge at its summit, so all the privileges of grace converge in prayer to God.[202]

Tapping into the resources of God's being is an experience longed for by every leader, particularly when facing a difficult problem. However, more

---

199 Roy Oswald, *Clergy Stress: A Survival Manual for Church Professionals and Clergy Burnout: A Prevention and Self-care Manual,* (Minneapolis, MN: Ministers Life Resources, 1982), p. 14.

200 Ralph A. Herring, *The Cycle of Prayer,* (Nashville, TN: Broadman Press, 1966). Cycle of Life is the name I have chosen to give to Herring's picture of how God works through prayer. Herring calls it a cycle of prayer. Herring also provides a somewhat unique view of the way in which prayer is a part of a larger redemptive cycle of God. God's redemptive cycle is the unfolding process through which God accomplishes His will in the lives of people and the world. Herring demonstrates with clarity the way in which prayer is a vital part of coming before God in such a way so as to participate in His plan.

201 Romans 11:33, 36, NIV.

202 Herring, *Cycle of Prayer,* p. 17.

often than not, it appears that many leaders struggle to find the answers and strength to cope with the obstacles they encounter in the ministry. The reason for their inability to deal with an issue or person may not be immediately clear, resulting in frustration and sometimes resignation to their foe. It is also possible and in many cases very likely that there are other specific reasons for the leader's struggle with prayer, especially if his prayers do not appear to be getting answered.

The Bible is quite clear on the fact that if one will commit his way to God, that God will gladly direct his life in accordance with the will of God.

> *Trust in the Lord with all your heart and lean not to your own understanding; in all your ways acknowledge him, and he will make your paths straight.*[203]

The scripture also identifies those things that serve as hindrances to an effective prayer life. Additionally, life itself verifies that an effective prayer life can be blocked by many types of attitudes, behaviors, sins,[204] theological and psychological fears,[205] problems, faith issues, and much, much more. It is not unreasonable to think that some of these very things plagued young Timothy as he attempted to deal effectively with the presence of Alexander.

Despite the obstacles and hindrances that one potentially faces when he commits himself to a ministry of prayer, a leader is often confronted by certain misconceptions about prayer. If accepted, these misconceptions could prevent a leader from experiencing the fullness and richness of prayer. In *Let Prayer Change Your Life,*[206] Becky Tirabassi identifies at least four reasons that prayer is sometimes set aside in favor of some other strategy for dealing with one's problems.

---

203 Proverbs 3:5–6, NIV.

204 See Hybels, chapter 7 and 8 entitled "The Mystery of Unanswered Prayer" and "Prayer Busters" in which he identifies a variety of things that a believer should check out when prayer goes unanswered: (1) the request may be inappropriate, (2) the timing may be off, or (3) there may be a problem in the life of the one who is praying. Other concerns include: (4) prayerlessness—James 4:2, (5) lack of persistence—Luke 18:18, (6) unconfessed sin—Isaiah 59:2, (7) unresolved relational conflict—Matthew 5:23–24, (8) selfishness—James 1:5–8. See also E.M. Bounds, *Purpose in Prayer* (Grand Rapids, MI: Baker Book House, 1920), p. 105–120.

205 Gary A Wilde, *Your Ministry of Prayer* (Elgin, IL: David C. Cook Publishing Co., 1990), p. 48–49ff. Wilde mentions these two reasons for ineffective prayers are worthy of investigation.

206 Becky Tirabassi, *Let Prayer Change Your Life: How You Can Release God's Power* (Nashville, TN: Thomas Nelson Publishers, 1990), p. 17–21.

Misconception #1: *"It's Boring." Sometimes prayer is considered boring due to the pure exhaustion that comes from a regular time of prayer. The person who accepts this point of view is often the one who fails to stay around and see the results of persevering in prayer. This person is excited about many of the other spiritual disciplines, yet they know little of the power that is released when one participates in true prayer. This person has never considered the fact that to disguise prayer as boring is exactly the thing that Satan would do in order to keep people away from this wellspring of power. Two final questions must be posed to the person who thinks that prayer is boring: Why would the disciples ask Jesus how to pray, rather than how to perform a miracle or carry out a healing? Also, if prayer was so boring, why did Jesus spend so much time doing it?*

Misconception #2: *"Prayer is Only for the Pious and the Spiritual." This misconception holds some truth, but we hold the key that unlocks the door. It is true that God will not listen and answer our prayer when we cherish sin in our hearts. However, the Bible tells us that through confession of our sin (1 John 1:9) we can open the doors to receiving his blessing in our lives. The point is clear concerning the misconception. It is by having a broken and contrite heart that one is able to come before the throne of God.*

Misconception #3: *"God Doesn't Always Answer Prayer." Whether one believes that God can or cannot meet one's need is largely dependent on how one perceives God. A lack of faith in anyone certainly decreases a person's ability to trust in that person. Believing in a God that doesn't perform miracles, bring the dead back to life, converts sinners, etc., is to believe in a God that is different from the God of the Bible. Therefore, it becomes one's personal faith to believe that prayer to God as validated in the Bible not only will be heard, but answered.*

Misconception #4: *"My Prayer Has No Power." This misconception is one more of ignorance than rebellion. We simply do not know the truth if we believe that prayer has no power. Ignorance about the power that is available through prayer automatically sets many believers into a powerless category of Christian living known as prayerlessness. Many have failed to* *perceive and experience prayer as a source of power due to the lack of a mentor who had experienced prayer in that very way, or there would be many more of us who love to pray.*

It is very unlikely that young Timothy accepted any of these misconceptions about prayer. One must remember that most of Timothy's leadership training had been spent under the capable guidance of the apostle Paul. There may have been believers in the first century that lived a "boring" life; however, based on the record of the Acts of the Apostles and his many epistles, Paul's life was anything but boring. Neither would one expect Timothy to believe the idea that prayer was only for the pious. Paul himself had struggled with the fact that within his own power he could not measure up to God's standard of righteousness (Romans 3:23; 7:7–25). Despite his shortcomings, Paul never backed away from encouraging his fellow-servants to pray (Colossians 4:2; 1 Timothy 2:12).

Paul believed without question in the fact that God answered prayer and that prayer was the lifeline provided by God to tap into his power. Otherwise, there would be no need to ask others to join him in prayer (Romans 15:30–33) or to demand that a young leader like Timothy be devoted to prayer in the midst of conflict and personal struggles (1 Timothy 2:13; 4:15). Certainly Timothy was blessed to have a mentor like Paul, who demonstrated a life of faithfulness in prayer and one who exhorted him concerning the importance of praying. There is little doubt that Timothy understood the nature of prayer and the impact that prayer can have on one's ministry, but what about the leaders of today?

The Dynamics of Prayer

In *The God Who Hears*, Bingham Hunter expresses a belief that the leaders of today struggle with the pain of feeling that God does not hear their prayers. Hunter suggests various reasons[207] for this belief. Most notable is his conviction that when leaders pray, they do not know what they are doing. This does not mean that there have not been many proposals throughout history as to the real meaning of prayer and much discussion on its importance and significance, writes Hunter, but that very few are willing to talk about what prayer is.

One only needs to participate in a traditional prayer meeting at the local church in order to see first-hand that many people, including pastors, continue

---

207 W. Bingham Hunter, *The God Who Hears*, (Downers Grove, IL: InterVarsity Press, 1986), p. 10–14. Hunter proposes a list of reasons why he thinks the leaders of today do not turn to prayer as they should.

to view prayer *as a way to get God to give them what they want.* Hunter notes that for this reason many leaders are susceptible to the latest technique or fad that comes along claiming to improve one's prayer life.[208] The result, however, is not favorable when a leader sees God as the quick fix-it man who eagerly waits to fill a list of demands. On the contrary, true prayer is not getting God to do one's personal bidding, but, rather, it is *"a means God uses to give us what he wants."*[209]

Prayer Possibilities and Principles

A man once remarked, "Example is better than precept." To put this truth another way, the best way to learn something is to watch someone else do it. Through the lens of scripture, one is able to observe men and women who serve as excellent models of what it means to be faithful in prayer.[210] Paul's life itself had become an example for Timothy to follow in the midst of caring out the daily responsibilities of the ministry. But what exactly were the possibilities for the ministry in Ephesus as Timothy set it apart in prayer? What principles did he follow in order to be in touch with the mind of the Lord and the instruction of the Word? Through a careful look at the Pastoral Epistles and other relevant biblical texts, one is able to identify exactly what it takes to be effective in prayer.

The leader who develops a prayer life that conforms to the standards of the Bible will make possible the transformation of his ministry and life for the glory of God. John Biersdorf, in an Alban Institute publication on prayer and ministry entitled *How Prayer Shapes Ministry*, comments on the transforming power of prayer in a leader's life by saying:

> *In the life of prayer, we can confront and transcend the patterns. In the long and patient sitting in the presence of God, the next step in our journey is discerned ....Our conscious notions of why we do what we do may have little relationship to those hidden images and rhythms. But in prayer the Spirit intercedes for*

---

208 Ibid., p. 11.
209 Ibid., p. 12.
210 For a closer look at the life of some of the most effective pray-ers in the scripture, refer to: (1) Abraham—Genesis 18:16–33; (2) David—2 Samuel 7:18–29; (3) Ezra—Ezra 9:1–15; (4) Jonah—Jonah 4:1–11; (5) Jacob—Genesis 32:24–30; (6) Hanna—1 Samuel 1:9–11; (7) Jehoshaphat—2 Chronicles 20:6–12; (8) Daniel—Daniel 9:1–19; (9) Habakkuk—Habakkuk 1:24, 12, 13 (10) Paul—Ephesians 3:14–21; (11) Jesus—Matthew 26:36–46. Other key biblical figures worth considering include: Moses, Elijah, Hezekiah, Nehemiah, and Samuel.

us with sighs too deep for words—so we may begin to discern
what we are to live out and what we need to let go of, what old
lives are dying and what new dreams of God's will are being
born.[211]

This was certainly true for young Timothy. Before charging into Ephesus and attempting to take control of the situation and the person of Alexander, Timothy would be expected to spend time in prayer in order to seek God's will both for his life and those for whom he ministered. Through prayer he would gain a heavenly perspective of what God wanted him to do in Ephesus and develop the spiritual perspectives that would enable him to transform his relationship with Alexander. Timothy would learn a tremendously important fact about prayer that every leader must learn if he ever expects to accomplish God's will for his life. He would learn that sometimes it is necessary for a leader to change before he is ever ready to assist in the growth or change in another situation and especially in the life of another person.

Prayer that Changes Things and People

Prayer can change things or people when a leader is committed to praying. The unfortunate fact is that many leaders do not consistently pray, thus forfeiting the power that is available to them at the throne of God. The very nature of the ministry is such that a leader is tempted to approach the demands of a busy schedule without ever spending time in prayer, either before, during, or after a particular experience.

Leaders who can identify with this approach to the ministry might be wise to ask why this pattern has developed in their lives. Could it be simply a matter of time? Certainly no one would argue with the fact that the ministry is time consuming and demanding in a variety of ways, but to argue that time to pray is not available, if only in small increments, would be unrealistic.

Perhaps it is more reasonable to suggest that a leader does not pray as he should in view of all the things that he must do. Is it possible that a leader could be led to think that prayer is not the most efficient way to spend his time, resulting in a substitution of other activities that seem to bring more immediate results than a commitment to prayer? In this case prayer is not a priority. Unfortunately, a change of priorities is unlikely unless a leader is willing to re-evaluate the teaching of the scriptures on the importance of prayer as well as reconsider the matter of how prayer can be more easily integrated into his thinking processes about the ministry.

---

211 John E. Biersdorf, *How Prayer Shapes Ministry*, (Washington, DC: Alban Institute Inc., 1992), p. 29.

Both of these proposed blocks to an effective prayer ministry on the part of a leader are possibilities. However, there is another alternative that must be considered as we think about the prayer life of the modern-day leader. A leader may be busy, and it is possible that a leader may have difficulty determining those tasks that must take priority over others. Nevertheless, a more fundamental question concerns the matter of faith. Does the leader actually believe that God is able to do all things?

A failure to pray as one should in the ministry is partly due to the fact that many times leaders would rather handle their difficulties on their own. On the other hand, a failure to turn to God in prayer may be closely tied to the fact that in effect one does not believe that God can handle the problem. This belief is clearly different from the teaching of the Bible, where page after page one can read testimony of how God answered the prayers of faithful men and women.[212]

Today, more than ever, God is looking for faithful men and women to come to him in prayer. He yearns for leaders to bring to Him their needs and the concerns they have for a person, even a difficult one. The only leader that will faithfully complete this task is one who believes that through prayer God is able. Bill Hybels appropriately describes this type of person as a "prayer warrior."

> *A 'prayer warrior' is a person who is convinced that God is omnipotent; that God has the power to do anything, to change anyone and to intervene in any circumstance. A person who truly believes this refuses to doubt God.*[213]

Prayer is often thought of in terms of the impact that it has on the subject of our prayers. It must not be forgotten, however, that one of the reasons that we struggle with prayer so often is the fact that we are human and our natural inclination is revenge or self-defense rather than reaching out to a brother or sister who needs our support.

It would be unrealistic to think that young Timothy did not struggle with the job of praying for Alexander. More than likely he would have preferred to get even with this man instead of bringing him before the throne of God to pray that his needs be met and to ask God to change his heart. Given this

---

212 Hybels, p. 27–37. In the chapter entitled "God is Able," Bill Hybels discusses the variety of ways in which the Bible demonstrates God's ability and faithfulness in hearing and answering the prayers of his people. Hybels mentions, among many ways, God's power over (1) nature; (2) circumstances; (3) lives, and much more.

213 Ibid., p. 35.

possibility, what could have caused Timothy to pray for Alexander with a commitment to see God work in his life as well as in the ministry of Ephesus? The answer may be found in the fact that in prayer God not only responds to our needs, but to us. Regarding this subject Bingham Hunter writes:

> *From a biblical point of view, prayer is related to everything that we are and everything that God is. God does not respond to our prayers. God responds to us: our whole life. What we say to him cannot be separated from what we think, feel, will and do. Prayer is communication from whole persons to the Wholeness which is the living God. Prayer is misunderstood until we see it this way.[214]*

For Timothy, prayer was a way to come face to face with God. Through this personal encounter in the presence of God, Timothy was given the opportunity to change.[215] According to one writer, if permitted, prayer can become a relationship through which God can dramatically alter one's entire view of life.[216] From a practical and realistic point of view, this must have been the experience of Timothy for him to be able to faithfully pray for Alexander.

Once a leader experiences the transforming power of God in his life, the possibility of an effective ministry is enormous. No longer will the leader be preoccupied with a pursuit of his personal needs, but a conscious and determined effort will be made to serve the Lord obediently. In the words of Henri Nouwen, "prayer becomes a time when the leader is enabled to move toward God and away from himself, resulting in a newness of life.

Prayer is a radical conversion of all our mental processes because in prayer we move away from ourselves, our worries, preoccupation, and self-gratification—and direct all that we recognize as ours to God in the simple trust that through his love all will be made new."[217]

How does this happen in the leader's life? In what way does this

---

214 Hunter, *The God Who Hears*, p. 13.

215 See 2 Corinthians 3:18, where Paul speaks of the transforming power of God in the believer's life. Paul uses the Greek word μεταμορφουμεθα, 1 person plural present indicative of μεταμορφοω meaning to transform. By coming to Christ in faith, we are set free to become more like him.

216 Becky Tirabassi, *Let Prayer Change Your Life*, (Nashville, TN: Thomas Nelson Publishers, 1990), p. 47–58. In this chapter, Tirabassi identifies at least four ways in which prayer changes a person: (1) priorities; (2) possibilities; (3) personality; and (4) perspectives.

217 Henri Nouwen, *Clowning in Rome*, (Garden City, NY: Image, 1979), p. 73.

transformation process begin and continue in the life of the leader and flow over into the results for his ministry? The answer is rather basic. By turning to the Word of God one can discover a set of clear *biblical principles* concerning prayer, which if followed, will guide a leader to a productive prayer life and a ministry that brings fruit for the kingdom of God.

Principles That Work

The apostle Paul admonished the believers in Thessalonica to "pray continually"[218] for the simple reason that he viewed prayer as an indispensable ingredient in the leader's spiritual arsenal when coping with conflict in the ministry. In describing the spiritual armor of the Christian soldier to the Ephesian believers, Paul also made mention of the importance of prayer by exhorting the saints to "pray in the Spirit on all occasions with all kinds of prayers and requests. With this in mind, be alert and always keep on praying for all the saints."[219] Obviously, Paul saw prayer as both essential for ministry and possible to carry out in the midst of even the most difficult ministry setting.

It would be hard to think of a committed leader not being a person of prayer. The demands of the ministry have a potent way of drawing one to that time and place of prayer in which the leader can find rest and receive direction for "battles" in the spiritual war that he must fight along the way. Charles Spurgeon, commenting in his classic book, *Lectures to My Students,* remarks that in his mind, "a minister (leader) *is always praying.*"

> *Whenever his mind turns to his work, whether he is in it or out of it, he ejaculates a petition, sending up his holy desires as well-directed arrows to the skies. He is not always in the act of prayer, but he lives in the spirit of it. If his heart be in his work, he cannot eat or drink, or take recreation, or go to his bed, or rise in the morning, without evermore feeling a desire, a weight of anxiety, and a simplicity of dependence upon God; thus, in one form or other he continues in prayer. If there be any man under heaven, who is compelled to carry out the precept—Pray without ceasing," surely it is the Christian minister. He has peculiar temptations, special trials, singular difficulties, and remarkable duties; he has to deal with God in*

---

218 1 Thessalonians 5:17, NIV. Greek αδιαλειπτως προσευχεσθε, translated "pray continually." Paul's point is clear. Believers are exhorted to continually be in a spirit of prayer.
219 Ephesians 6:18, NIV.

awful relationships, and with men in mysterious interests; he therefore needs much more grace than common men, and as he knows this, he is led constantly to cry to the strong for strength, and say, 'I will lift up mine eyes unto the hills, from whence cometh my help.'[220]

In view of this, one final task remains in the consideration of the role of prayer and conflict in the local church. Each principle must be examined by a leader in order to gain a sufficient grounding in the teaching of the Word and a sense of direction for his own personal journey along the path that will prayerfully lead the church back to health.

Principle Number One: Patiently Waiting in His Presence

Turning to God for rest, strength, and direction in the midst of those "special trials" was a common practice of King David. Despite his wealth, status, and more significantly his power to manipulate his conditions, he discovered that it was only in and through prayer that he could find hope (Psalm 62:1), stability (Psalm 62:2b), rest (Psalm 62:5), protection (Psalm 62:6), love (Psalm 62:12), and reward for faithfulness (Psalm 62:12) in the midst of troubling times.

For David, as well as for many other biblical men and women prayer was a time of waiting in the presence of the Lord.[221] Sitting in silence was the beginning of the leader's journey to understanding the Lord's will in a particular situation. While praying may be common for some leaders, it is not always a fruitful time. At times, it can be heard among believers that "God never seems close when I pray," or someone may ask, "Does God really hear me when I pray?" Regardless of these feelings of abandonment that face every leader at one time or another, God is always near, and it is this sense of God's nearness that David longed for more than anything else.

Whom have I in heaven but you? And earth has nothing I desire besides you. My flesh and my heart may fail, but God is

---

220 Charles Spurgeon, *Lectures To My Students,* (Grand Rapids, MI: Zondervan Publishing House,, 1954), p. 42.

221 A passage like Psalm 40:1 supports the importance of waiting for the Lord. In Psalm 62:1, David speaks of the rest God gave him. In verse 5, David challenges himself to continue to rest in God. *The New American Standard Version of the Bible* translates Psalm 62:1 as: "My soul waits in silence for God only." This translation would suggest the importance of sitting before the Lord in silence in order to hear the Lord when he speaks to his servant.

the strength of my heart and my portion forever. Those who are far from you will perish; you destroy all who are unfaithful to you. But as for me, it is good to be near God. I have made the Sovereign Lord my refuge, I will tell of all your deeds.[222]

Being near to God and listening in silence for Him gives the leader an opportunity to hear the Lord as He comes to him. The apostle James viewed this as the way in which the believer can invite the Lord into his presence. He reveals this when he said: "Come near to God, and he will come near to you."[223] In view of this, what actually happens when the leader patiently waits in the presence of the Lord?

Leaders must come before the Lord in order to renew their strength that is so often drained in the midst of conflict. While leaders work with limited resources, God is seen in the scriptures as the source of strength and power (Isaiah 40:29). By coming to the Lord and waiting patiently in His presence, God will renew His servant with strength from on high.

Yet those who wait for the Lord will gain new strength; they will mount up with wings as eagles, they will run and not get tired, they will walk and not become weary.[224]

Charles Swindoll, a noteworthy twenty-first century leader, suggests that this passage in Isaiah argues for the means by which a leader can find relief from his worries and weariness.[225] By patiently waiting for the Lord to lead, a leader is given that which is needed for any problem he may face. Isaiah's description of what takes place in the believer's life when he comes into the presence of the Lord indicates that the power of this encounter with the Lord in silence is capable of meeting our deepest need. This brings us to a final question regarding principle number one. Why should a leader wait in the presence of the Lord? In the words of Swindoll, we wait because as leaders we don't have the ability to deliver ourselves from conflict, the stability to hang secure in the midst of life's storms, the hope to fight the discouragements that are almost commonplace in the ministry, or the ability to provide refuge from the attacks of people and the impact of a constant onslaught of problems. In essence, we are hopeless without God. Therefore, we must accept the exhortation of the scriptures to wait on the Lord.

222 Psalm 73:25–28, NIV.
223 James 4:8a, NIV.
224 Isaiah 40:31, *New American Standard Version*.
225 Charles R. Swindoll, *Three Steps Forward, Two Steps Back*, (Nashville, TN: Thomas Nelson Publishers, 1990), p. 80–81.

Wait for the Lord; be strong and take heart and wait for the Lord.[226]

Principle Number Two: The Power of Perseverance

Principle number one emphasized the power that is available to the leader who faithfully enters into the presence of the Lord through prayer. Principle number two indicates the importance of staying in the presence of the Lord long enough to hear His response. The importance of obeying these prayer principles is demonstrated in the lives of men and women throughout the scriptures, but perhaps nowhere more clearly than in the lives of Nehemiah and the persistent widow. Through a brief look at the experiences of these "prayer warriors," a leader will learn about the potential that is available to bring about change in the midst of conflict.

Nehemiah

In the year 445 BC , Nehemiah first heard the news about the Jewish remnant living in Jerusalem after the exile. According to Nehemiah 1:1, he lived in the citadel of Susa when he heard the news that the Jews were experiencing great "trouble and disgrace," and that the city and its wall were in ruins. Although Nehemiah was distressed to the point of mourning, he immediately turned to the one task that he knew could bring results. He prayed.

Nehemiah's prayer was more than simply a request to God for help! His prayer was a combination of **adoration** ("the great and awesome God" Nehemiah 1:5); **requests** ("let your ear be attentive and your eyes open to hear the prayer your servant is praying … " Nehemiah 1:6); **confession** ("I confess the sins we Israelites, including myself have committed against you" Nehemiah 1:6b); **a reminder of God's promises** ("I will gather them from there and bring them to the place I have chosen as a dwelling for my Name" Nehemiah 1:9); and, arguably the most significant characteristic, **persistence** ("praying before you day and night for your servants, the people of Israel" Nehemiah 1:6).

Nehemiah's persistence in prayer can be seen in the fact that four months had passed from the time he first heard about the needs of his fellow Jews to the point when he brought his concern before the King (Nehemiah 1:1; 2:1). The decision of Nehemiah to pray on the behalf of his people would seem to be a very natural response for a leader in the midst of conflict, but the key to his success and ultimately for every leader was to continue in prayer even when an answer did not seem imminent.

---

226 Psalms 27:14, NIV.

Nehemiah also exhibited persistent prayer in the face of opposition. Nehemiah 4:78 indicates that as soon as progress was being made on the wall intense opposition arose against Nehemiah and his company of builders. This is often true for leaders when confronted by those who see that progress in the ministry is taking place. Like the opponents at the wall who came to "... stir up trouble...." (Nehemiah 4:8), the leader is often confronted by difficult people who are determined to sabotage the work of the ministry. The potential for resolving these kinds of problems is still the same and can be seen in Nehemiah's response, "But we prayed to our God."[227]

The Persistent Widow

The Old Testament principle of being persistent in prayer was also taught by Jesus to his disciples. As he often did, Jesus used a parable to make his point about the importance of *praying and not giving up*.[228] Through the story of a widow who would not stop seeking the help of an unjust judge against her adversary, Jesus illustrated the power of crying out to God both "day and night."[229]

A leader who has to contend with a difficult person day after day can also find comfort in these words. According to Jesus, there is untapped power in the commitment of a person to continually come before the Lord in prayer. By always praying,[230] a person (leader) makes a strong statement of faith in God's promise to meet his need. The power of such a prayer is not to be seen in the persistence of the widow or in the leader, but rather in the caring response of a loving God over against an angry and unjust Judge whose actions are motivated by his own lack of care and impatience. The persistence of the one who prays demonstrates to God that he truly wants to hear the Lord's response.

---

227 Nehemiah 4:9, NIV.

228 Luke 18:1. Greek μη εγκακειν, present active infinitive of εγκακεω, meaning to never to become weary or tired, lose heart; with μη subject infinitive of δειν.

229 Luke 18:7, NIV.

230 William D. Spencer and Aida B. Spencer, *The Prayer Life of Jesus*, (Lanham, MD: University Press of America, 1990), p. 42. The Spencers note the particular way in which Jesus used the adverb "always" by placing it in front of the verb rather than afterwards. It is their belief that Jesus did this in order to emphasize the fact that the disciples should not become weary in praying because God is different than the unjust Judge. Jesus is proclaiming that God cares and will meet his promise to meet their need provided they "always pray."

A Modern Day Dilemma

The experience of the ministry suggests that prayer is often one of the most neglected spiritual disciplines. The ministry can be a very busy lifestyle, implying that perhaps part of the reason for the neglect of prayer is simply that it is perceived to be a waste of valuable time, especially if the leader does not receive immediate and tangible results. In the most extreme cases, a leader may view prolonged times of prayer as an inefficient way of dealing with conflict. Nevertheless, the Bible teaches that the opposite is true, for it is only in prayer that the leader will find strength and direction needed to cope with conflict.

The experience of Paul and Timothy in Ephesus provides sufficient evidence of the importance of prayer for carrying out a successful ministry. Prayer was important to Paul, and he did not hesitate to challenge Timothy with high expectations regarding the task of praying for one's work in the church and one's relationships with the people of the church, particularly those who might be considered difficult. The challenge that was placed before Timothy concerning prayer is the challenge that comes to every leader as he seeks to effectively carry out the work of Christ.

In this chapter, I have presented information about the potential power of prayer in the life of a leader. The leader must apply this understanding to his own life in a practical way in order to see how God will honor His word and be true to His character. I believe that although God is working in and through the church today, much more could be accomplished if God's people and especially his leaders would pray.

Once again it must be understood that prayer is only one phase in a series of steps that a leader must take in order to deal effectively with a difficult ministry situation or person. In chapter one, I emphasized the importance of being prepared when called upon to face conflict in the church. This preparation included understanding the background of the difficult person, as well as many other "contexts of influence" that play a significant role in the formulation of a difficult person's approach to life. Following a time of careful preparation, the leader is challenged to keep his head in the midst of a tough situation so as not to misjudge the need or make a hasty move in an effort to solve the problem.

In chapter three I have suggested that prayer is the key that will unlock the door of potential to effective problem-solving. Being prepared and keeping one's head are necessary, but it is often because of prayer that God is able to take a leader's faithful work and transform these ingredients into a plan of action that will meet the need of the situation.

In chapter four, I discuss the importance of seeking the reconciliation and restoration of a difficult person. Again, throughout the process it will be important for the leader to remember the importance of prayer in determining the will of the Lord. Through a time of waiting and persistently coming before the Lord, an acceptable plan can be chosen and implemented.

Our final task is to move beyond prayer, although we will never cease to pray (1 Thessalonians 5:17), and formulate a plan of intervention that is acceptable to our understanding of the situation and need. There are many plans of intervention already in existence today and each possesses positive traits. However, it is my opinion that no one plan is adequate for all needs. Therefore, it is important for the leader to examine the strengths and weaknesses of each plan under consideration and choose the plan that is best suited for the problem that is being addressed.

If, after a leader has an understanding of these guidelines and principles, he is committed to carrying them out, the church will in most cases move forward in the process of dealing with a difficult person in a way that pleases God and brings the best results possible for those involved in the conflict.

Dealing with a difficult person is almost never an easy task but one that is absolutely necessary. Leaders will struggle at times in this task, but the potential benefits for the people of God are tremendous and more than worthy of our best efforts!

Chapter Four
Jesus, Paul, and Difficult People

The New Testament books of 1 and 2 Timothy demonstrate the importance of trusting God through difficult times. The probability of facing opposition in the ministry was a truth learned long ago by the apostle Paul and was communicated to Timothy in an effort to help him understand the dynamics and realities of the pastoral ministry (2 Timothy 3:12). The fact that Timothy faced opposition in Ephesus should come as no surprise.

The apostle Paul was well acquainted with the potential for opposition as one tried to preach a gospel that was contrary to the ways of the world. This, however, was secondary to the fact that the gospel was the vehicle through which Paul would experience the grace of the Lord. It was because of God's grace that Paul entered into the pastoral ministry (2 Timothy 1:9–10) and through his grace that Paul would endure its struggles.

Experiencing conflict in the ministry was nothing new for the apostle Paul. In fact, the gospel itself was seen as the reason for which much of Paul's suffering took place (2 Timothy 2:9a).

> Remember Christ Jesus, raised from the dead, descended from David. This is my gospel, for which I am suffering even to the point of being chained like a criminal.

For some, suffering is the prelude to failure, but to Paul it was a necessary part of serving God in a hostile world. In Paul's mind, suffering was a powerful way in which God brings a leader face to face with his own inability to control the ministry. Fortunately, he is also confronted with the fact that God is able to bring victory through any circumstance, regardless of how difficult it may seem.

This was the attitude displayed by the apostle Paul while writing to the Philippian church from a prison in Rome.[231] While serving time in prison for his defense of the gospel (Philippians 1:13–14), Paul was confronted with the fact that there were those who viewed his imprisonment as a deterrent to the advance of the gospel. This, however, was not Paul's opinion. On the contrary, Paul believed that despite his circumstances, God was advancing the gospel.

> *Now I want you to know, brothers, that what has happened to me has really served to advance the gospel. As a result, it has become clear throughout the whole palace guard and to everyone else that I am in chains for Christ.*[232]

Paul's imprisonment served as a perfect opportunity for those who supported and opposed him to take action. The text indicates that while many of the brothers began to preach the gospel "courageously and fearlessly,"[233] others took advantage of Paul's condition and preached only in an effort to "stir up trouble ..." for him.[234] Nevertheless, Paul maintained a confident spirit in the midst of these difficult times. His confidence came not from his own strength, but from the prayers of others and the abiding presence of God's Spirit. Paul's number one concern in the midst of conflict was not his own welfare. His priority was the effective preaching of the gospel. If this could be done, Paul was more than satisfied (Philippians 1:18–19).

Paul's concern for the effective preaching of the gospel is best demonstrated by his own desire to be faithful when confronted with persecution. His desire for faithfulness was anchored in a deep love for God and a strong yearning for the Philippians to grow in that same love (Philippians 1:9–11). By being faithful to God in the midst of persecution, Paul exercised his belief that God would honor his commitment to him and ultimately lead to his deliverance (Philippians 1:19). However, it must be noted that Paul was a realist. Paul

---

231 Philippians 1:12–21. *The NIV Study Bible: New International Version*, (Grand Rapids, MI: Zondervan Bible Publishers, 1985), p. 1801. Scholars suggest that the evidence points to a Roman imprisonment, yet some are intent on arguing for an imprisonment in either Ephesus or Caesarea. A Roman imprisonment appears to fit better with the last chapter of Acts (28:14–21). It would appear that he was under house arrest, unlike his condition during the writing of 2 Timothy.

232 Philippians 1:12–13, NIV.

233 Philippians 1:14, NIV.

234 Philippians 1:17, NIV.

was also aware of the possibility that God might choose not to deliver him. This too was perceived by Paul as an opportunity for Christ to be exalted in his life.

> *I eagerly expect and hope that I will in no way be ashamed, but will have sufficient courage so that now as always Christ will be exalted in my body, whether by life or by death.*[235]

Paul's advice in Philippians 1:27–28a reveals his greatest concern for the ongoing work of the ministry.

> *Whatever happens, conduct yourselves in a manner worthy of the gospel of Christ. Then, whether I come and see you or only hear about you in my absence, I will know that you stand firm in one spirit, contending as one man for the faith of the gospel without being frightened in any way by those who oppose you.*[236]

Paul's desire for the believers in Philippi to be faithful in the face of conflict and suffering is best viewed against the backdrop of his own understanding concerning Christ's teaching about persecution. For Paul, it was not only expected that believers will encounter persecution as they live out their faith,[237] but that each believer should respond to conflict and suffering in a way which would bring glory to Christ and mirror the attitude of Christ to those around them (Philippians 2:1–5).

Paul was convinced that the faithful endurance of believers in the midst of persecution could be used by God for His glory. This is the reason Paul was not overly concerned about his confinement in a prison. Though he was physically held in prison by chains,[238] Paul knew that the Word of God was not chained.[239]

---

235 Philippians 1:20, NIV.

236 Philippians 1:27–28, NIV.

237 Philippians 1:29, NIV.

238 2 Timothy 2:9. Paul describes himself by using the word κακουργος, nominative singular masculine adjective of κακουργος, ον meaning criminal or evildoer. This word is used only one other time in the New Testament. Luke uses this word to describe the criminals that hung on the crosses beside Jesus during his crucifixion (Luke 23:32–33, 39). In 2 Timothy, this term is used to suggest a stricter form of imprisonment (Kelly, p. 177), rather than the house arrest condition which Acts 28 seems to suggest.

239 2 Timothy 2:9. Greek δεδεται, 3rd person singular perfect passive indicative of

for I am suffering even to the point of being chained like a criminal. But God's word is not chained. Therefore I endure everything for the sake of the elect, that they too may obtain salvation that is in Christ Jesus, with eternal glory.[240]

The Model of Jesus

Paul's view of Christ can be seen not only in the words he said but in the way he lived his life. Through a closer look at the life of Jesus, one is able to discern a model upon which Paul patterned his behavior. In chapter two of the book of Philippians, the attitude of Christ is revealed as one of *humility*, a character trait that was absolutely essential for the apostle Paul as he dealt with his adversaries and equally important for the leader of today who wants to deal effectively with opposition in the ministry.

The humble attitude that was "fleshed out" in the life of Jesus is especially remarkable. When it is remembered that Jesus willingly submitted himself to the persecution of men, even unto death on the cross (Philippians 2:8b), the problems experienced by man seem insignificant. According to Jesus and Paul, regardless of the reason for a leader's opposition, the best way for a leader to handle persecution is to do "nothing out of selfish ambition or vain conceit, but in humility consider others better than yourselves."[241]

This attitude demonstrated by Jesus and Paul toward persecution and opposition in the ministry was first taught in the New Testament by Jesus to the disciples.

Blessed are you when people insult you, persecute you and falsely say all kinds of evil against you because of me. Rejoice and be glad, because great is your reward in heaven, for in the same way they persecuted the prophets who were before you.[242]

δεω, meaning to bind or tie. See also 1 Thessalonians 2:13 for another reference by Paul in which he refers to the Word of God as powerful and always at work in the lives of those who believe. See Kelly, p. 178, for the idea that by using this statement, Paul wants to get across to Timothy the idea that the very sufferings that he is talking about have a positive evangelistic significance. Paul realizes that there are those who have not yet heard the gospel or responded to it; therefore, he endures the suffering in a positive way, hoping and praying that God will use it to reach lives.

240 2 Timothy 2:9–10, NIV.

241 Philippians 2:3, NIV. See also Galatians 5:20, where selfish ambition is listed among the acts of the sinful nature. For Paul, to act in humility was the best thing a person could do to maintain or bring about the unity of the body.

242 Matthew 5:11–12, NIV. See also Luke 6:22–23.

It is extremely important to observe that Jesus did not say that everyone who experiences persecution will be blessed. Jesus did, however, indicate that persecution was to be experienced by his disciples in two ways: (1) it must be undeserved "falsely say all kinds of evil against you … " (Matthew 5:11), and (2) the persecution must be "because of righteousness" (Matthew 5:10). In conclusion, Christ declared that obedience to this command accomplishes two worthy goals: (1) it ensures the believer of the highest reward for "great is your reward in heaven … " (Matthew 5:12), and (2) it identifies the believer with the greatest men and women throughout biblical history by declaring "in the same way they persecuted the prophets … " (Matthew 5:12).

The exhortations found in the Sermon on the Mount (Matthew 5:1–12) are considered by some to be unrealistic. It is argued that the expectations of these teachings are too high to reach and perhaps are intended for another age. If permitted, a similar argument could be made for the Ten Commandments (Exodus 20:1–5 and Deuteronomy 5:6–21). This, however, cannot be accepted. It is exactly at this juncture that the Sermon on the Mount and the Ten Commandments have importance and power for the believer. These sets of commands were not given by God in order that one might have a way to meet God's expectations. On the contrary, they were given to demonstrate one's inability to meet God's standards and to emphasize the fact that each person needs God's son, Jesus Christ, the Savior.

The benefits of abiding in Christ and obeying his word result in the blessedness of the believer.[243] This word means more than happy, and suggests the ongoing spiritual joy of the believer who is obedient to Christ and a fellow-heir to the kingdom of God.[244]

> *Now if we are children, then we are heirs-heirs of God and co-heirs with Christ, if indeed we share in his sufferings in order that we may also share in his glory.*

The believer is never blessed by pursuing his own desires, but by following a path of commitment to Christ despite the fact that he may experience conflict

---

243 Matthew 5:3ff. Greek Μακαριοι from μακαριος, ια, ιον. This word is used in reference to man while another New Testament word, ευλογητος (cf. Luke 1:68), is often used in praise of God. See I. Howard Marshall and W. Ward Gasque, *The New International Greek Testament Commentary: The Gospel of Luke,* (Grand Rapids, MI: William B. Eerdmans Publishing Company, 1978), p. 248–249, for a discussion of the importance of these two words. See Bauer, p. 487, for a more detailed look at the way in which this word is used in the scriptures.

244 Romans 8:17, NIV.

and suffering. The blessing comes when he receives insults,[245] persecution,[246] and false accusations[247] because of Christ (Matthew 5:11).

The command[248] of Jesus to endure persecution of this nature is extremely important for the leader when one considers the opposition he faces in the ministry. Does this command imply that the leader is forever at the mercy of those who persecute him? After the leader has prepared himself and prayed for his oppressor (Matthew 5:44), is there ever a time when he must move beyond the persecution and attempt to confront his adversary? The answer to this pastoral dilemma is yes; however, the leader must proceed according to the guidelines provided by the scriptures.

Guideline Number Three: Seek Reconciliation

The importance of being prepared for confrontation in the pastoral ministry cannot be overstated. The nature of the ministry itself suggests that there will be many times when a leader is challenged over his convictions and actions. In many situations, an immediate confrontation between the pastor and his opponent would only complicate the situation and prohibit movement toward a satisfactory resolution. By delaying the choice to intervene, the pastor is given an opportunity to spend quality time in focused prayer[249] on the matter at hand. Through prayer, the leader intentionally gives God time to work.

---

245 Greek ονειδισωσιν, 3rd person plural aorist active subjunctive of ονειδιζω, meaning to reproach, revile, or heap insults upon someone. See 1 Peter 4:14 for a description of how blessed it is to go through suffering because of one's love for and commitment to Christ.

246 Greek διωξωσιν, 3rd person plural aorist subjunctive of διωκω, meaning to persecute. See also 2 Timothy 3:12 for the idea that anyone who wants to live a godly life will be persecuted. See Philippians 3:14 and Bauer, p. 200, (διωκω) for examples when this word means to hasten, run, or press on.

247 Greek Ψευδομενοι, nominative plural masculine present participle of Ψευδομαι, meaning to lie or tell a falsehood. See passages like Romans 9:1; 2 Corinthians 11:31; Galatians 1:20; Colossians 3:9; and 2 Timothy 2:7 for passages that use a form of this word. See Bauer, p. 900a, for further information on the biblical usage of this word.

248 1 Peter 4:14–15 reiterates the teaching of Matthew 5 that the persecution experienced by believers must be undeserved in terms of committing a crime, but deserved in terms of one's commitment to Christ. Peter declares that the person who is insulted because of Christ is blessed "for the Spirit of glory and of God rests on you" (vs. 14). If able to suffer for Christ, the believer should consider himself blessed to bear his name (Christian).

249 I addressed the importance of prayer in the midst of conflict in chapter three. At this juncture, it will suffice to say that prayer is the key to many unanswered questions in the ministry. In Matthew 7:7–8, Jesus said, "Ask and it will be

On the other hand, experience has proven that there are times when a leader must immediately intervene in a situation of conflict if there is to be any hope of resolution. The reasons for conflict are many. The intensity, however, though it may vary, usually depends on two factors: (1) the people involved and (2) the reason for the conflict.

It is the second factor that Jesus focuses on when advising his disciples on the importance of handling conflict in a loving and caring fashion (Matthew 18:15–20). The instructions found in Matthew 18 are considered by many to be the biblical model of confrontation to be used by the church when attempting to restore a brother who has fallen out of step with the walk of the faith. Few would argue with this point; however, it seems very likely that Jesus was not only providing a guideline for confrontation but an explanation of what the leader, or church, must do when reconciliation cannot be achieved.

In this sense, Matthew 18:15–20 serves as one of two extremes in the New Testament that are worth discussing regarding biblical confrontation. The other extreme is discussed by Paul in 2 Corinthians 2:5–11. These texts are quite clear on the role of the leader with regard to handling conflict. In Matthew, Jesus provides the leader with specific directions on how to deal with a person who rejects all attempts to reconciliation. In 2 Corinthians, on the other hand, Paul addresses the task of receiving a person back into the church that has been reconciled (2 Corinthians 2:5–11). A proper understanding of each extreme will provide the leader with a solid foundation upon which he can build an effective plan of intervention.

Matthew 18:15–20

In Matthew 18, Jesus gives his disciples a series of teachings about what it takes to be a part of the kingdom of heaven and how those who are a part of the kingdom should live.[250]According to Jesus, kingdom living includes the

---

given to you; seek and you will find; knock and the door will be opened to you. For everyone who asks receives; he who seeks finds; and to him who knocks, the door will be opened". See Charles R. Tarr, *Prayer: An Enjoyable Experience*, (Anderson, IN: Warner Press, Inc., 1986), p. 29ff for his discussion of four principles of effective prayer that emerge from this passage. They are as follows: (1) We must simply ask; (2) We must ask specifically; (3) We must ask fervently; and (4) We must pray trustingly.

250 Matthew 18:1–4 teaches the importance of humility in the Kingdom. Jesus likens the process of getting into the kingdom to becoming like a child. According to Jesus, child-like faith is a leading characteristic of the members of the kingdom of God. Matthew 18:10–14. In this text, Jesus speaks of the loving care of God through the imagery of a shepherd who goes to look for one lost sheep, even though ninety-nine remain safely in the fold. Jesus uses this illustration to make

development of a child-like faith (vs. 16), a caring attitude for those who are lost (vs. 10–14), the willingness to be reconciled with those who are at fault (vs. 15–20), and the practice of forgiveness (vs. 21–35). One cannot miss the emphasis in these passages on the need for a believer to humble himself if he wants to be a vital part of the kingdom experience.

The practice of humility is especially important for the leader who wants to minister effectively to a difficult person. This is the type of person Jesus speaks of in Matthew 18:15–20 when he advises his disciples on the importance of seeking reconciliation with a brother who sins against them. The fact that Jesus uses the word sins[251] is significant in pointing out the difference between a brother who simply disagrees with a person and one who intentionally seeks to harm or discredit someone through his actions.

The idea of going to a brother who has sinned against you to show him his fault is not a pleasant thought for any leader. Perhaps this is the reason the apostle Paul designated this kind of task for those who are considered to be mature in their faith (Galatians 6:1). Jesus emphasized that this kind of confrontation is best carried out "just between the two of you" (Matthew 18:15). According to Jesus and Paul, if the act of confrontation is carried out in the right spirit, there is the possibility that the brother will respond favorably and be reconciled (Matthew 18:15).[252]

Timothy's task in Ephesus included the work of correcting, rebuking,[253] and encouraging those who no longer put up with sound doctrine (2 Timothy 4:2). Paul encouraged Timothy not to get involved in "foolish and stupid arguments … " (2 Timothy 2:23) since that approach "is of no value, and only ruins those who listen" (2 Timothy 2:14). Instead, Timothy was to gently

---

the point that God is a loving God and does not wish for anyone to perish (18:1–4). Matthew 18:15–20 continues the idea of caring for those who are in trouble by talking about a brother (or sister) who has fallen into sin and is in need of reconciliation to those he has offended. Like God, the person who was offended needs to make every effort to bring about the reconciliation of this fallen "out of grace" person. The final text in this section is found in Matthew 18:21–35 and is known as the parable of the Unmerciful Servant. This parable is a result of Peter's question about forgiveness. Jesus responds by telling his disciples through the use of a parable that if you want to be forgiven, you must forgive others.

251 Matthew 18:15. Greek αμαρτηση, 3rd person singular aorist active subjunctive of αμαρτανω, meaning to sin.

252 Greek ελεγξον, 2nd person singular aorist active imperative of ελεγχω, meaning to reprove, correct, or point out. See Bauer, p. 249–250 for a variety of meanings associated with this word. See passages like Luke 3:19; John 3:20; 16:8; Ephesians 5:11, 13; and 1 Timothy 5:20.

253 Greek ελεγξον.

instruct those who opposed him in the ministry (2 Timothy 2:24–25) in order that they might "come to their senses and escape from the trap of the devil, who has taken them captive to do his will" (2 Timothy 2:26).

The manner in which a leader goes about the task of confronting a difficult person is critically important to the ongoing life of the church. Based on Jesus' use of the word ελεγξον, as well as its use and meaning in other New Testament passages,[254] it can be determined that the goal of confronting a person with his fault, even if it is sin, is not to humiliate, anger, or potentially ostracize him, but to create an environment in which he will listen.

The advice of Jesus on this matter is filled with great wisdom. This can be seen clearly in the fact that Jesus expected the one who is offended to go to offender *alone*. This is not what one would normally expect. Today, it is often considered appropriate for the offender to come to the one who has been offended and present assurance of sorrow for the offense and make acceptable apologies.   Yet, this is not what Jesus has instructed a person to do when he has been offended by the sins of a fellow brother.

There is a distinct advantage for the leader who chooses to initiate reconciliation with a fallen brother. First, it avoids unnecessary waiting. It is possible that the leader will be disappointed when the offender does not come to him in order to clear up a problem. Secondly, the leader will lose a valuable opportunity to demonstrate a forgiving spirit to a brother if he does not make the first move toward healing a broken relationship.

The reason this approach has so much power is in the fact that it models the love of the Father toward mankind. John the Apostle writes concerning this love, "This is love: not that we loved God, but that he loved us and sent his Son as an atoning sacrifice for our sins" (1 John 4:10). In this verse one can see the fact that God did not wait for us to come to him, but He comes to us in order to move us toward reconciliation (2 Corinthians 5:17–20). John also reveals that the Lord's method of confronting humankind is loving and personal. John states:

> *This is how God showed his love among us: He sent his one and only Son into the world that we might live through him.*[255]

This approach is repeated in Jesus' instructions regarding confrontation with a brother who is caught in sin. The leader is exhorted to go to the brother alone in hopes that he will listen. Jesus suggests this approach, indicating that a private meeting will go far to alleviate any misunderstandings and potentially

---

254 Other New Testament passages support translations like expose, bring to light, convince, or convict. See Bauer, p. 240–250, for further information.
255 1 John 4:9, NIV.

rekindle the dynamics of a healthy relationship. Should this approach fail, the leader should take "one or two others along, so that every matter may be established by the testimony of two or three witnesses."[256]

Again, there is wisdom in the approach of the Master. By taking along one or two friends during a second trip, the leader is able to strengthen his influence on the life of the offender. The presence of one or more witnesses also ensures the reliability of the testimony about what takes place during the leader's visit with the brother. It is possible that even after a leader's second attempt to reconcile the offending brother to him, there will be no signs of repentance or reconciliation. In this case, Jesus exhorts the leader to take the entire matter to the church (Matthew 18:17).

If a leader's effort to bring about reconciliation reaches this point, there is evidence that either the approach to confrontation has erred or that the offender is unwilling to change his heart and mind on the matter. The command to bring the matter before the church is not intended to bring humiliation, but serve as a means of bringing the entire church body into the process of bringing about the reconciliation of the fallen brother. Through informing the church body, the offender can be prayed for and admonished by other believers in an effort to bring him back to his spiritual senses. The informing of the church body about the behavior of a fallen brother also served as a warning to those who might for some reason follow his example. The practice of rebuking a brother who had sinned was to be used by Timothy in order to warn others against following this type of behavior (1 Timothy 5:20).

Depending on the response of the offending brother, it is at this point in a leader's approach to confrontation that his strategy may take a turn in another direction. If the brother refuses to listen to the counsel of the church body concerning his sin, the church is instructed to treat him "as you would a pagan or tax collector."[257]

It is here that one is able to see the potential power of the church body led by a faithful leader when following the commands of the Lord. Jesus declares:

---

256 Matthew 18:16, NIV.

257 Matthew 18:17, NIV. Tax collectors were not well thought of in the first century. The NIV Study Bible suggests that tax collectors were hated and considered traitors. Tax collectors worked for the Roman tax contractors, whose job it was to collect taxes from the people. Tax collectors often took this an opportunity to collect more money than necessary in order to pay off Rome and save some for themselves. Pagans: the believer was not expected to spend time with a pagan since becoming a member of the church. In the same way, Jesus instructs the believers not to fellowship with a fallen brother if he/she fails to repent and be reconciled to the church body.

I tell you the truth, whatever you bind on earth will be bound in heaven, and whatever you loose on earth will be loosed in heaven. Again, I tell you that if two of you on earth agree about anything you ask for, it will be done for you by my Father in heaven. For where two or three come together in my name, there I am with them.²⁵⁸

In these verses found in Matthew 18:18–20, Jesus encourages the believer, the leader, and the church body to follow his instructions. The reason is simple and worth hearing. By following the Lord's instructions concerning the confrontation of a fallen brother, the church has available the power to secure at least three things: (1) divine approval of its behavior; (2) a complete answer to its requests; and (3) a personal fellowship with its Lord.²⁵⁹

Jesus' final words here have tremendous value for the faithful leader in his attempt to bring about healing in the church body by seeking reconciliation with a brother who has sinned. Three powerful principles are set in motion through the obedience of a leader and church body to the Lord's instructions regarding confrontation.

Principle #1. *The church is the vehicle through which God is carrying out His will on earth. Therefore, whatever the church decides²⁶⁰ to do on earth will be acceptable to God in heaven if done in accordance to His revealed plan.*

Principle #2. *The church has available untapped resources in heaven. If the church can agree on what to do in the midst of any situation, and if it is based on a clear leading of the Holy Spirit, God will do exactly what is asked of Him.²⁶¹*

---

258 Matthew 18:18–20, NIV.

259 These three potential achievements of the church are provided by David Thomas, (ed.) and William Webster, *The Gospel of St. Matthew: An Expository and Homiletic Commentary*, (Grand Rapids, MI: Baker Book House, 1956), p. 363ff.

260 Jesus uses two words in combination to make his point in Matthew 18:18. Jesus uses a form of δεω and a form of λυω, which are translated respectively "forbid" and "permit." See Bauer, p. 177, and Joseph Henry Thayer, *A Greek-English Lexicon of the New Testament*, (New York, NY: American Book Company, 1889), p. 131, for a further discussion on the use of these two words in the New Testament and early Christian literature.

261 See Philippians 4:23. In this passage, Paul admonishes Euodia and Synthyche to agree. In a book that focuses on the importance of unity in the midst of

Principle #3. *The church is an instrument of God's power and the reservoir of His presence. Wherever God's people join together, even a small number (two or three), God is present there in the midst of them (Matthew 18:20). The church can accomplish great things if it is willing to draw upon the strength of the Lord.*

Every attempt at reconciling a fallen brother will not be successful. However, without obedience to Jesus' plan of confrontation, all is potentially lost. At times, a leader will face a difficult person who is virtually untouchable. Like the hypocritical leaders in the day of Timothy, he doesn't respond due to the fact that he has lost all sensitivity to what is right or wrong (2 Timothy 3:7). Nevertheless, the faithful leader will make every effort to restore such a brother to the church body. If successful in reconciling the fallen brother, the church takes a significant step forward in the battle against Satan, whose number one goal is to entrap the believer in his sin.

Matthew 18:15–20 is a very important passage when seeking to develop an understanding of the Bible's teaching on effective confrontation. Nevertheless, it is only part of the total picture. Hopefully, a fallen brother will be reconciled through a careful and loving ministry of confrontation. If so, what then is the responsibility of the church body to this person in order to make sure he is completely restored to the fellowship of the saints? Our second passage, found in 2 Corinthians 2:5–11, provides everything needed for a biblical approach to this task.

Guideline Four: Seek Restoration

– *2 Corinthians 2:5–11*

The pastoral ministry can be very difficult at times. One of those times is during the process of confronting a difficult person with his sin.[262] This was true for the apostle Paul in his ministry to the people of Corinth. In his first letter to the Corinthians (1 Corinthians 5:1–5), Paul reminds the Christians of

---

suffering and persecution, one can see the importance that Paul lays on agreeing in the Lord.

262 The apostle Paul usually followed a pattern of "gentle persuasion" (2 Timothy 2:25). However, there were those times that Paul became unwilling to accept a certain behavior (i.e., Galatians 1:8–9). In this particular case, Paul was against those who taught a different gospel from the one he had preached. Most of the time Paul is the one who is determined to do all that is possible not to offend or turn away a brother.

the fact that he had passed judgment on a man who was behaving in a sexually immoral manner. In fact, in 1 Corinthians 5:9 Paul reveals that he had already written the Corinthians about this problem in a previous letter.[263]

In 2 Corinthians 2:1–4, Paul indicates that he had written another letter besides 1 Corinthians and the letter mentioned in I Corinthians 5:9. He also mentioned that he had made a second visit to Corinth, which was very painful (2 Corinthians 2:1). The fact that this visit was the second visit by Paul is confirmed in 2 Corinthians 12:14 and 13:2 where the apostle speaks of his plans to make a third visit to Corinth. The reason why the visit was painful for the apostle is made known in 2 Corinthians 2:5–11. From all indications, the apostle experienced some kind of opposition during his second visit to the city of Corinth that caused him deep distress and great anguish of heart (2 Corinthians 2:4).

The hope of every leader is to see the positive results of confrontation. In 2 Corinthians 2:5–11 Paul makes every effort to ensure that the Corinthians did not bypass their opportunity to turn an act of confrontation into an experience of growth and joy for the entire church body.[264] Apparently, during Paul's second visit to Corinth he had experienced opposition from a certain person who was probably a part of the church. This seems likely since Paul was now writing the believers in Corinth encouraging them to welcome this man back into the church as a result of his repentance, not to mention having been punished for his sins.[265]

The decision to punish this man was made by a majority of the people in

---

263 Obviously, we know about 1 Corinthians, but there is evidence in 1 Corinthians 5:9 that Paul had written a letter prior to what we know as 1 Corinthians in which he had warned the Corinthians about associating with sexually immoral people who were part of the church body. Also, it has been argued based on 2 Corinthians 2:3–4 that Paul wrote another letter known in some circles as the "intermediate" letter. The letter was considered intermediate in the sense that it was written sometime between the writing of 1 and 2 Corinthians. According to the NIV Study Bible footnotes on page 1764, some have identified it with the last four chapters of 2 Corinthians, either in whole or in part, suggesting that they do not fit will with the first nine chapters.

264 2 Corinthians 7:8–12 reveals the fact that Paul was glad that even though he had to be hard on the Corinthians during this entire ordeal of dealing with an offender in the church, the result was a positive one. The Corinthians eventually were led to the point of repentance, perhaps in their willingness to tolerate the presence of such a person. This act of spiritual pride was present in the case of the sexually immoral brother mentioned in 1 Corinthians 5:1–5, unless of course, these two accounts are referring to the same person.

265 Possibly some form of excommunication based on the information received in 1 Corinthians 5:5 and 1 Timothy 1:20.

the church. The fact that Paul mentions majority implies that the decision was not unanimous. This, however, is not surprising in that many times decisions are made in the church that are not necessarily in agreement with everyone's desires. In this case, it would seem probable that Paul was in agreement with the decision of the church to punish the man for his behavior. However, Paul was also aware that the church is not simply a type of spiritual court handing out sentences on those who violate the law of God, but also a community of grace. Therefore, in an attempt to bring healing into a situation filled with pain and hurt, Paul admonishes the Corinthian church to welcome this man back into the body.

The goal of any church body when disciplining a person who has sinned is restoration. It is always possible that the person who is receiving the discipline will not respond in such a way that will permit a satisfactory resolution to the problem. However, Jesus reminds us that "if he listens to you, you have won your brother over" (Matthew 18:15b). The Corinthian church had been obedient to the challenge of effectively carrying out confrontation with a brother who was at fault; nevertheless, their task was not complete. Just as the Corinthian church had been faithful in holding this man accountable for his behavior, Paul instructed them to forgive and comfort the brother, in addition to reaffirming their love for him (2 Corinthians 2:7).

Forgiving,[266] comforting,[267] and reaffirming your love[268] for a person who has offended you is an enormous task for any person who fails to accept these characteristics as being at the heart of God's plan for effective ministry in the church. Paul's purpose in asking the Corinthian church to accept the brother in this way is made clear in verse seven of chapter two. Paul realizes that the unwillingness to give forgiveness, comfort, and love to a person who truly wants to be reinstated to the fellowship could lead to disaster, both for the

266 Paul uses the Greek word χαρισασθαι, an aorist middle infinitive of χαριζομαι meaning to forgive or pardon. See Bauer, p. 885a, for a further study of his word and its use in the New Testament. The aorist tense is used by Paul in this case to indicate action as occurring. See H.E. Dana and Julius R. Mantey, *A Manual Grammar of the Greek New Testament,* (New York, NY: The McMillan Company, 1948), p. 193ff, for a further discussion of the use and importance of the aorist tense. See Benjamin Chapman, *New Testament Notebook* (Grand Rapids, MI: Baker Book House, 1977), p. 69, for the idea that Paul might be using the aorist in an epistolary sense. The aorist is used in this way when the author views a future action as past (i.e., forgiven, comforted). Another usage might be the culminative (this aorist may have in view the end of the action; Chapman, p. 69. The middle voice is used to emphasize the subject as participating in the results of the action (Dana and Mantey, p. 157). The use of the infinitive in this passage is a little more difficult to determine. It seems most likely that Paul is using the infinitive in the sense of command; however, there are those who suggest that Paul uses the infinitive here in the sense of result. See Dana and Mantey, p. 215–216, for a discussion of the infinitive. See also Fritz Rienecker, *A Linguistic Key to the Greek New Testament Vol. 2: Romans-Revelation,* (Grand Rapids, MI: Zondervan Publishing House, 1980), p. 110, for the idea that Paul uses the infinitive in the sense of result. However, I believe that the idea of command seems more consistent with the test in that Paul declares "you ought to forgive and comfort him … " (2 Corinthians 2:7).
267 Greek παρακαλεσαι, an aorist active infinitive of παρακαλεω, meaning to comfort, encourage, or cheer up. The active voice is used here by Paul to emphasize the action of comforting (Dana and Mantey, p. 157).
268 Greek κυρωσαι, aorist active infinitive of κυροω, meaning to affirm, reaffirm, confirm. Paul uses the infinitive in this verse (vs. 8) as an infinitive if indirect discourse. The indirect discourse use of the infinitive is introduced by words of saying, thinking, seeing, hearing, perceiving, etc. In this case, Paul uses the word "urge" to introduce the infinitive. Paul is seen here as asking the congregation to make some kind of action toward the brother to affirm the start of a new relationship. The fact that this word was commonly used with a legal connotation can be seen in Paul's use of the word in Galatians 3:15 (hapaxlegomenon, apart from 2 Corinthians 2). In this passage, Paul points out that "no one can set aside or add to a human covenant that has been duly established …." With this in mind, 2 Corinthians 2:8 would suggest the idea of a formal vote or ratification by the church to re-admit the repentant offender back into their fellowship.

person and the church body. In the case of the brother, without forgiveness, he could be led to the point of being "overwhelmed[269] by excessive sorrow"[270] (2 Corinthians 2:7).

Paul's insistence on forgiving the offending brother may have come partially from the fact that it was in Corinth that some had opposed his apostolic authority. As a result of that opposition, Paul may have been prompted to test[271] the Corinthians in this process of confrontation and restoration regarding their commitment to doing what was right (2 Corinthians 2:9). Beyond this, Paul had a greater purpose in mind when he commanded the Corinthians to forgive and restore the fallen brother. In Paul's mind, the lack of forgiveness opened the door for Satan to enter into the fellowship of believers. Therefore, Paul suggests that whenever a brother falls, the church must do everything possible to restore that person to the fellowship of the church. If this is not done as quickly as possible, Satan can get his foot in the door and use this failure to outwit the fellowship of believers.[272]

---

269 Greek καταποθη, 3rd person singular aorist passive subjunctive of καταπινω, meaning to swallow up or overwhelm. Paul is apparently concerned that the way a church disciplines a fallen brother is not so inflexible that it sets up a limit on the grace of God. The idea that the church's behavior could "swallow up" a person is clearly seen in such passages as: Matthew 23:24; 1 Corinthians 15:54; 2 Corinthians 5:4; Hebrews 11:9; 1 Peter 5:8.

270 Greek μη πως τη περισσοτερα λυπη. μη πως, a conjunction denoting purpose. The NIV translates it "so that" (2 Corinthians 2:7). The KJV translates it "lest perhaps ...." τη περισσοτερα dative singular feminine comparative adjective of περισσοτερος, τερα, ον meaning greater or more. λυπη dative singular feminine of λυπη, ης, η, meaning grief, pain, or sorrow. Paul is concerned that if the church does not receive this fallen yet repentant brother back into the church that he will be overcome with sorrow over his situation. This must be coupled with the fact that Paul is of the conviction that the punishment had been sufficient (Greek ικανον, 2 Corinthians 2:6). See Philip Edgecumbe Hughes, *Paul's Second Epistle to the Corinthians*, (Grand Rapids, MI: William B. Eerdmans Publishing Company, 1962), p. 66–67, for the idea that the word translated "sufficient" in 2 Corinthians 2:6 is a simple Latinism (=satis; cf. Luke 22:38 ικανον εστιν, and Mark 15:15, το ικανον ποιησαι=satisfacere).

271 Greek δοκιμην, accusative singular feminine of δοκιμη, ης, η, meaning approved character, test, ordeal. In this context, this word serves as a direct object of γνω (meaning to know). Paul wanted to make sure that the Corinthians had successfully gone through the entire process of bringing a person from the point of confrontation to complete restoration into the church body.

272 2 Corinthians 2:11. Greek πλεονεκτηθωμεν, 1st person plural aorist passive subjunctive of πλεονεκτεω, meaning to take advantage of, outwit, defraud, or cheat. A form of this word appears also in 7:2 and 12:17. Paul also uses the word νοηματα, accusative plural neuter of νοημα, ατος, το , meaning purpose,

It is conceivable that after every attempt to bring healing into a situation of conflict by a leader, a satisfactory resolution will not be found (Matthew 18:15–20). However, the goal of conflict resolution is one of complete restoration. Provided this happens, it is hoped that a church will not struggle to accept a fallen fellow believer back into the church fellowship (2 Corinthians 2:5–11).

A Final Look (2 Timothy 2:7)

The need for an effective plan of confrontation was exactly what Timothy needed as he considered the task of carrying on the work of the ministry in Ephesus. Such a task as this has many obstacles, but none so challenging as the work of confronting a difficult person like Alexander (2 Timothy 4:14–15). Yet it is in view of this environment that Paul admonished Timothy to pass on the essence of the gospel, even if this meant having to confront problems. In fact, at the heart of Paul's advice was an exhortation to work hard, even to the point of enduring hardship (2 Timothy 2:3).

Throughout this book, the importance of exercising patience has been emphasized. The practice of patience was particularly important for a young leader like Timothy, who did not possess the depth of experience equal to that of his mentor the apostle Paul. Nevertheless, Timothy had sufficient experience in the ministry to know that by listening to Paul and heeding his advice, he would be able to carry on the work of the Lord in Ephesus.

The years of working with Paul in the ministry had taught Timothy many

---

design plot, thought, or mind as the direct object of αγνοουμεν, 1ˢᵗ person plural present active indicative of αγνοεω, meaning not to know, or to be ignorant. Paul uses the subjunctive to emphasize an objective possibility. By using the subjunctive, Paul shows that even though the verbal idea is not now a fact, it may become one. The action is possible, but it depends on certain objective factors. For Paul, the most important factor is that of forgiveness. The passive is used to show that the believer who does not forgive will be outwitted. Elsewhere in this epistle, Paul uses this word in the sense of the mind or understanding of man: 3:14, 4:4, and 11:3, and once of every thought or purpose: 10:5. Its only other occurrence in the New Testament is in Philippians 4:7. The fact that Satan is interested and busy seeking for opportunities to "outwit" believers can be seen in passages like Luke 22:31 and 1 Peter 5:8–9. Satan is also busy blinding the spiritual eyes of unbelievers so they cannot see the light of the gospel (2 Corinthians 4:4). While writing to the believers in Ephesus, Paul encourages the believers to not give Satan an opportunity to use things like unresolved anger as a means to get his "foot" into the door of the church. If permitted to get his foot into the door of the church or into a person's life, there is little chance to become the kind of church body that God desires (Ephesians 4:27).

things about being an effective leader. He not only learned the importance of patience in the midst of conflict, but he had experienced the power that comes into a leader's life when he spends time with God in prayer prior to addressing a problem. Through patience and prayer, Timothy was able to prepare himself for that time when he must actually confront the conflict in Ephesus face to face.

The time will eventually come for every leader, as it did for Timothy, when he will have to experience that "necessary confrontation."[273] The importance of being prepared for his time of confrontation is absolutely essential if he hopes to bring healing into a situation that is plagued with conflict. Being prepared, however, is only part of the task. The leader must not only be prepared with the necessary information[274] that will aid him in understanding the conflict but know how to approach a particular situation of conflict in the most effective way,[275] so as to bring about the best possible results for everyone involved.

Problem-Solving with a Purpose

A wise man once said, "There's always more than one way to look at things." The leader who desires to be an effective problem solver would do well to listen to these words of advice. Remembering that each person is different and worthy of being heard will go far in transforming a relationship that is "stuck" into one that is characterized by trust and cooperation. This is especially important when one realizes the significance of communication to the task of dealing with conflict. When two people are unable to communicate in a

---

273 See Judson Edwards, p. 172f, for my thoughts on when confrontation is necessary: (1) When a person is doing something that is consistently making us angry, (2) When a person is doing something that is hurting other people, and (3) When a person's behavior is damaging himself. Edwards adds that there are at least three approaches that a leader must adhere to if confrontation is going to be successful and move a situation toward resolution: (1) confront directly, (2) confront thoughtfully, (3) confront kindly.

274 Each pastor should build a profile of how a difficult person might tend to act in the midst of a conflict situation. This will prove to be helpful information for the leader who wants to have a good grasp on the way in which a difficult person might act and why.

275 Tim Hansel, *Eating Problems for Breakfast,* (Dallas, TX: Word Publishing, 1988). In this book, one will find a wealth of practical information on the art of problem solving. Hansel has a unique way of approaching this sometimes burdensome task of dealing with problems. For anyone looking for an innovative way to add creativity to your problem solving abilities, Hansel's book is a must read.

way that will permit growth and understanding, resolving conflict is very unlikely.

This idea is endorsed by James Fairfield in *When You Don't Agree,* by suggesting the thought that "A good relationship is a two-way communication."[276] Unfortunately, experience indicates that much of the communication taking place in the home and church today falls far short of this desired goal. On the contrary, people are busy pursuing the fulfillment of their own agendas. Conflict occurs when one person's agenda clashes with that of another.

The fact that people are in conflict with one another should come as no surprise. According to Les Giblin, there is something "deep in the heart of every man and woman that is important and demands respect."[277] In fact, notes Giblin, "the most powerful drive in any person is to maintain this individuality, to defend this important something against all enemies."[278] In language almost too difficult for some to accept, Giblin describes all people as "egotists" at heart.[279] The fact that people are determined to uphold their

276 James G. T. Fairfield, *When You Don't Agree,* (Scottsdale, PA: Herald Press, 1977), p. 236. Fairfield presents in this chapter "six equal rights" that need to be honored if effective and caring communication is going to take place. With each right, there is a corresponding equal right: (1) I will respect your right to be equally hear/I will claim my right to be equally heard, (2) I will respect your ownership to your side of the dialogue and refuse to carry on both sides by myself/I will own my sole responsibility for my side of the dialogue and refuse to let you speak for me, (3) I will stop myself from speaking to my image of you and not demand that you be what you were or what I want you to be/I will not try to match your image of me, I am free to change what I was and choose who I will be, (4) I will not anticipate your responses/I will not bait a reaction from you, (5) I will expect no more than a clear statement of your views and feelings/I will not withhold or distort my views and feelings, (6) In no way do I want to hamper your freedom for you to be truly you when you are with me/In no way do I want to squander my freedom for me to be truly me when I am with you. By following these guidelines alone, a leader will enhance his ability to calmly work through a conflict.

277 Les Giblin, *How To Have Confidence and Power in Dealing With People,* (New York, NY: The Benjamin Company, Inc., 1956), p. 12.

278 Ibid, p. 12.

279 Ibid, p. 13. In the process of describing people as egotists, Giblin lists four characteristics of all people: (1) We are all egotists, (2) We are all more interested in ourselves than in anything else in the world, (3) Every person you meet wants to feel important and to "amount to something," (4) There is a craving in every human being for the approval of others, so that he can approve of himself. In view of this, it is no surprise that Giblin argues that the best way to deal with a trouble maker is to help him feel better about himself (p. 17).

end of the perspective makes the task of bringing about change in the life of another person, especially a difficult one, a tremendous challenge.

Despite the fact that people are different, as leaders, we are still called upon to bring about positive change.[280] This is the essence of conflict resolution.

Choices that Change Lives

There are many models of intervention available today. Some models are based primarily on the importance of understanding a person's personality,[281] while others tend to focus on the importance of identifying certain behavioral signs that signal the presence of conflict.[282] On the other hand, there are those who believe that by following a simple process of gathering the right information and asking the right questions, a leader can solve most problems.[283] Still others suggest that if a leader understands his personal conflict style and reaction tendencies in the midst of conflict that all will lead to a satisfactory resolution.[284]

These particular models represent only a few of the most prominent approaches to dealing with problem people. With so many options available for the leader of today, one would think that nothing else is needed. This, however, is not an acceptable conclusion, nor one that agrees with the scriptures.[285]

---

280 Judson Edwards, p. 80–82. Here Edwards presents a variety of ways in which the common person attempts to bring about change in another person. Edwards makes it clear that each of these approaches fall short of being able to accomplish the change that is required if a conflict is to be resolved. These approaches include: (1) The **Halo Technique**—the idea of elevating self and lowering another; (2) **The Doghouse Technique**—informing someone that we are offended by something he's done; (3) **The Mirror Technique**—reflecting back to people exactly what they give us; (4) **The Tantrum Technique**— erupting into hostility when you do not get your way; (5) **The Public Flogging Technique**—embarrassing someone publicly.

281 See especially the literature produced by authors Francis Littauer and Tim Lahaye.

282 See Kenneth Haugk for an accurate presentation of this approach to conflict resolution.

283 Edward Hodnett, *The Art of Problem-Solving: How to Improve Your Methods*, (New York, NY: Harper & Row Publishers, 1955).

284 Refer to Fairfield and Hinkle for more details regarding the importance of identifying one's particular conflict management style.

285 The Bible has many examples of how leaders have dealt with the presence of difficult people and difficult situations. I would suggest that one refer to the word done by Dr. David Thomas entitled "The Church Faces Conflict," which was prepared for the Doctor of Ministry program at Gordon-Conwell Theological

Each plan of intervention available today provides at least some insight into the task of ministering effectively to a difficult person. Nevertheless, without an accurate and diligent[286] handling of the Word of God,[287] a leader will always fall short of what is needed to become all that he can become in Christ (2 Timothy 3:17).

The final step in processing the material in this book and the first step in learning how to apply the principles of *The Alexander Antidote* is to work one's way through the study guide. I have written this material in such a way that it would be most effective when shared by a pastor and his leadership team. My advice is to go slowly and be careful to maximize your interaction with this material. The results will be evident to everyone, as your team will become confident and well-positioned as leaders who handle conflict in a biblical and Christ-like way.

There is no greater responsibility or privilege given to a leader than that of being used by God to bring people together under the Lordship of Christ. Sometimes this involves dealing with difficult people. Nevertheless, it is a task that cannot be avoided, nor should it be set aside for something else that is more appealing. It is a work that demands a leader's utmost attention and one that cannot be neglected without harming the work of the kingdom. **To each leader who commits himself to this great task, "grace be with you" (2 Timothy 4:22).**

Seminary in South Hamilton, MA, in 1986. In this work, you will find four excellent sermons written by Dr. Thomas that deal with various situations of conflict during the time of the New Testament.

286 2 Timothy 2:15. Here Paul uses the Greek word σπουδασον, 2nd person aorist active imperative of σπουδαζω, translated to be zealous or eager, take pains, make every effort or diligent.

287 See William H. Willimon, *Preaching About Conflict in the Local Church*, (Philadelphia, PA: The Westminster Press, 1987) for the role that preaching can serve in dealing with conflict in the church.

Study Guide

Countless pastors and leaders expend enormous energy trying to lead the church but are regularly stymied in their attempts due to the presence of conflict. Conflict can arise due to many factors. A pastor may be ill-equipped or trained to handle it, the leadership surrounding the pastor may be reluctant to work toward resolving the problem and advocate tolerance, or an absence of any clear plan to respond to the conflict biblically are only a few of the reasons that conflict blocks the maturing and growth of the church.

What is needed is a way for leaders, especially pastors, to proactively prepare for and carry out a biblical and practical plan for resolving the conflict. This study guide has been created and designed to address this need. By working through this material, a pastor and his/her leadership team will be better equipped to respond appropriately to any situation.

This study guide is based on the book *The Alexander Antidote* , therefore its questions and exercises are based on the biblical account of Paul the apostle and his writing to his young apostolic delegate, Timothy. The entire guidebook takes into consideration both the historical context of the scriptures and the contemporary situation faced in the local church of the twenty-first century.

The goal of this work is simple. By working your way through this biblical teaching, it is hoped that each pastor and leadership team will be able to move the church toward health and be better able to deal with conflict the next time it arrives.

How to Best Use This Study Guide

For Pastors: After reading the book, at least a chapter at a time, this study guide would be best used as a tool that could be worked through with a core group of leaders in the church (i.e., elders). If not elders, then a selected group of people within the church that are interested in developing a plan for effectively responding to and developing a proactive strategy for handling conflict in the ongoing ministry of the local church.

For Church Leaders: After reading the book, at least a chapter at a time, a group of leaders in the local church would benefit the most by entering into a covenant with their pastoral leadership to work together through the study guide in order to develop a proactive plan for responding to and dealing effectively with conflict in the church.

For Pastors and Church Leaders: Once an agreement is made as to how this guide will be used, the leadership core of the church should plan when, where, and for how long they will meet to work through the study guide for the book. It will be very important to maintain a consistent schedule of meeting in order to maximize the benefit that could be gained through this exercise.

General Format of Study

Prior to the Meeting: make sure that everyone has read the appropriate chapter in the book.

- This study was developed on the idea that the senior pastor would serve as the facilitator for the study group.
- The facilitator should read over carefully the study guide sheet prior to the meeting to see if there are tasks that need to be accomplished prior to the group getting together.

At the Time of the Meeting: Open the meeting with prayer and specifically pray that God would give the group discernment and wisdom as they consider the material.

During the Meeting: Do not worry about being too structured. Work your way through the material and know that if more time is needed, it can be discussed at the next regularly scheduled meeting of the group.

- Have the facilitator begin by helping the group clarify the teaching of the chapter under consideration.
- Determine as a group with the help of the material what the author is saying and what is being asked of the group in response.

Once the point is clear ...

- Talk about the issue as it relates to your particular ministry setting. How is the issue affecting the health and vitality of your ministry?
- What does the author suggest as a remedy?
- How might this remedy be applied to your own setting? Be specific.
- Clarify after much discussion what you are thinking as a group in terms of application of the proposed remedy.

Pause for a moment ...

- Take this opportunity to spend time in focused prayer over this matter and ask God specifically for guidance.
- Following the time of prayer, collectively discuss whether or not God is changing anything previously discussed concerning this chapter's issue and remedy.
- Determine among the group whether or not something is changing as a result of prayer.
- Decide whether or not the subject needs to be tabled until the next meeting so the members can pray and think about what God might be saying to you as a group.

Take Action

- If the group is not sensing a change, talk about what you believe needs to happen in order for the remedy to be applied to your ministry.
- What specific steps of action need to take place in order for you to move forward in the book?

Close in prayer and remind the group of the next meeting's time and place.

Introduction

– *Summarize*

1. Facilitator: share with the group your thoughts about the *Introduction* to the book.

2. The author states that there can be many sources of conflict in the life of the church, ranging from bad theology, ministry practices, and even people.
   a. Identify as a group the areas in which your church has struggled in these three areas (be specific).
   b. Talk about any misconceptions that may have existed in the church as to how these problems would get resolved. Have they worked? If not, what has happened as a result of tolerating their presence?
   c. Group: The author states clearly that some problems exist due to the presence of a difficult person. Is this true for your church? If so, in confidence, identify those in your church who would qualify for this tag being put on them.

– *Discussion*

1. The author states that the remedy for resolving conflict is at least four-fold:
   a. Understanding the dynamics of preparation
   b. Balancing one's perception with reality
   c. Importance of exercising patience
   d. The significance of prayer

5. Discuss as a group:
   a. How prepared do you feel to confront conflict in a healthy manner?
   b. Does your perception of the problems in your ministry match reality? Have you done your homework and checked out whether reality matches your perceptions?

    c.   How patient are you? Should you slow down and take a deep breath before launching into trying to fix the problem? If so, what could you be doing to exercise patience?

    d.   Have you really prayed over this matter? What have you been praying? How often? Has God responded to your prayers? What is he saying into you? What is he saying to your group?

— *Prayer*

1. Stop right now and spend some time in prayer as a group.

2. Before you begin to pray, talk as a group about what you are seeking from the Lord regarding the issues you are praying about.

3. Following a time of concerted prayer, discuss as a group what you are sensing from the Lord. Is this a time for patience, or should you move ahead?

— *Closing*

1. Take time to determine what God is saying to you as a group.

2. Make a decision about moving ahead. Do you need to linger on the *Introduction* one more meeting? Set the date, time, and place of your next meeting.

3. Remind the group members to read *Chapter One* and pray about the meeting. Close in prayer.

Chapter One, Part 1: Understanding the Problem

— *Summarize*

Facilitator: share with the group your thoughts about your understanding of *Chapter One*.

1. The author argues that one of the major similarities between the first and twenty-first century church is the culture in which each exists.
   a. Review the definition of culture and society in this chapter.
2. The author states that societies can be broken down into smaller units called *subcultures* and that out of these emerge what are called norms or expected patterns of behavior.
3. In order to identify the norms of a given church, one must take a closer look at the subcultures that exist within the church.

— *Discussion*

1. Facilitator: remind the group of the *five* subcultures that the author identifies and work together in describing these for your church.
2. Assign members of the group to work individually or together to come up with a description of each subculture. NOTE: This may require some research either prior to holding this meeting or work to be done before this particular meeting can continue.

   The subcultures are as follows:

   - Historical
   - Familial
   - Pastoral
   - Theological
   - Geographical/Sociological

3. Group: talk about the findings in your research, making sure that the information collected and shared is accurate. Together,

create a draft of your conclusions that communicates your understanding of the subcultures within your church.

– *Prayer*

1. Take time now as a group to pray over your findings. Ask the group if there is anything in your findings that concerns you to the point that you need to pray over it.

2. Discuss as a group what you sense about your findings, feelings, and focus on these matters at this time.

– *Closing*

1. Before leaving, make plans to write up your thoughts for further consideration between now and your next meeting, which will be Part Two of your discussion of *Chapter One*.

2. Remind the group members to re-read the section of *Chapter One* entitled *Understanding the Person and the Problem* before the next meeting.

3. Set the date, time, and place of your next meeting. Close in prayer.

Chapter One, Part 2: Understanding the Problem

— *Summarize*

Facilitator: review with the group the discussion in the book of the ways in which conflict is usually experienced:

    a.   Intrapersonal conflict

    b.   Interpersonal conflict

    c.   Substantive conflict

1. Group: make certain that each of you understands the distinction between these types of conflict.

2. Group: following up on your group discussion concerning *subcultures,* decide as a group what kind of conflict has most often been experienced within your church. Once you decide, identify the top three areas of conflict and place them under the heading of one of the three categories.

— *Discussion*

1. If you identify at least one *substantive* type of conflict, determine the type of conflict that has caused the most turmoil within the life of the church

    a.   Over facts

    b.   Over methods or means

    c.   Over ends or goals

    d.   Over values

2. Determine as a group the level of difficulty for your particular conflict.

    a.   Problem to solve

    b.   Disagreement

    c.   Contest

    d.   Fight/Flight

    e.   Intractable situation

− *Prayer*

1. Pause at this point in the meeting to spend some valuable time in prayer as a group over what has been discovered during this meeting. Make sure everyone understands the scope of what you are praying about at this time.

2. After a time of purposeful prayer, talk as a group about what everyone is sensing about the challenges the group expects to face as they tackle the handling of the problems that exist in the church.

3. Determine together the most concerning conflict being experienced by the church. Close in prayer, asking God to guide you as a group/church in responding to the conflict.

− *Closing*

1. Reflect on your journey so far as a group, noting the things that you are learning about the hard work of handling conflict.

2. Make the assignment for the group of reading the remainder of *Chapter One,* beginning at the section called *Understanding the People in the Ministry Setting.*

3. Make clear the date, time, and place for the next meeting.

4. Close in prayer.

Chapter One, Part 3: Understanding the Problem

– Summarize

The author states that every leader eventually discovers people called by Carl George "EGR's" (Extra Grace Required Persons) who challenge them in their ministries. Marshall Shelly calls them "Well-Intentioned Dragons." Talk as a group about whether or not any EGR's exist in your church. NOTE: this is not a bashing exercise, so please proceed with caution as you discuss the matter as a group.

1. Facilitator: once an EGR is identified, discuss as a group the term "tender collision" used by Judson Edwards to describe how one must work with this type of person.
   a. This may be hard, but at this time the group should discuss whether or not the present leadership in the church has demonstrated the ability to turn a relationship with the difficult people in the church into a tender collision.
   b. Facilitator: have the leadership respond to the evaluation of the group and carry on a discussion about how the leadership can take steps to become better equipped in this area.

– Discussion

1. Group: discuss the proposed criteria and characteristics listed at the end of *Chapter One* that one must consider when preparing a workable plan for dealing with any kind of conflict in the church.
   a. Biblical
   b. Flexible
   c. Informative
   d. Directional
   e. Empathetic
   f. Interpretive

– Closure

1. Make certain that everyone in the group understands the bare essentials to each criteria and characteristic listed above. This is

something that we will return to later in our journey through the study guide.

– *Prayer*

1. Join together as a group at this time to pray over your experience during this meeting. Ask God to guide each member personally and the group as a whole in the development of a workable plan for handling conflict within the life of the church. Make clear to everyone that this is when the real work begins. Pray that God will give each member of the group clarity of thought, a spirit of understanding with regard to each other, and patience in the process.

2. After a meaningful time of prayer, ask the group to commit to reading through the entire books of 1st and 2nd Timothy in preparation for the next few meetings.

Closing

1. At this point in the study guide, it is possible that the group might be getting weary. Please take time to encourage each other in the process.

2. Make sure that everyone knows the date, time, and location of the next meeting.

3. Close the meeting in prayer.

Chapter Two, Part 1: Finding Balance in the Storm

– *Summarize*

Facilitator: lead the group in a discussion of the situation in Ephesus. Pay special attention to all of the dynamics going on in the Ephesian conflict. How important was Timothy's character in the mind of Paul when it came to responding to the persecution that might come from a leader's attempt to deal with conflict? Be sure to have a clear and accurate understanding of what is meant by "character"

1. Paul made it clear (1 Timothy 6:20) that his young apostolic delegate (Timothy) would have to guard the good deposit (gospel essentials) from those who would suggest that other things are more important in the particular context of ministry. What had become more important in Ephesus than the preaching of the gospel? Catalog your thoughts for further consideration.

– *Discussion*

1. Take time to consider as a group those things that have at times become more important in your ministry context than being obedient to the fulfillment of the Great Commission. Prioritize as a group and determine that which is or could become the most difficult to deal with as a church.

2. Sometimes the ministry itself can become a hindrance to being able to adequately address a potential or present problem. Revisit the author's discussion of decisions (Major, Moderate, and Minor) in this chapter that Timothy had to make in Ephesus, and talk with each other about the decisions that might need to be made in your ministry context if you are going to address the problem at hand. Work toward agreement on this matter. It will be important as you move forward in the Study Guide.

3. The author discusses the task of separating the *person* from the *problem*. Make sure that as a group you are seeing the problem and the proposed action accurately. Discuss as a group the difference between perception and reality. Is it possible that those things you are seeing at this point as a reality are perceptions that do not match reality?

— *Prayer*

1. This type of discussion can weigh heavy on your heart and mind. Take time now and do not hurry this step to pray over your conclusions. Ask God for clarity and confirmation on the major decisions that need to be made when confronting the present conflict that exist in your ministry context or a problem that you believe might be developing.

2. Following a time of directed prayer, talk openly about what you think God is saying to the group about the major, moderate, and minor decisions that need to take place.

3. Agree as a group about your collective understanding of the reality of your situation and take time again to pray.

— *Closing*

1. Facilitator: to prepare for your next meeting, have the group commit to reading the remainder of *Chapter Two,* beginning with the section entitled *Christ-Centered Principles.*

2. Set the date, time, and place for your next meeting.

3. Conclude your meeting with prayer.

Chapter Two, Part 2: Finding Balance in the Storm

— *Summarize*

Facilitator: it is time for the entire leadership group to take a deep breath and relax but not forget about the process they are working through. In order to get to a desired state, the group must continue to work through all of the issues and steps that are necessary to satisfactorily bring resolution to conflict.

As a group, rent and view together the classic movie *12 Angry Men*. This movie will raise a number of questions about how a group arrives at an accurate and truthful decision that needs to be made. Following the movie, consider how the experience of this twelve-man jury corresponds to the group's journey thus far through the study guide.

— *Discussion*

1. As a group, work toward agreeing on those things that have helped you move toward a clear understanding of what the problem is and what your response should be as leaders.

2. Begin the process of drafting a "white paper" on where your ministry stands right now in terms of health. Pinpointing the areas that must be addressed and made matters of prayer is the next major phase of developing a biblical and practical plan for resolving conflict.

— *Prayer*

1. Pause right now as a group and ask the Lord for patience, discernment, and guidance in the days ahead as you map out how you as a leadership team and church will prepare for the potential of and response to the presence of conflict.

— *Closing*

1. Ask the entire group to read *Chapter Three* in the book as preparation for the next meeting.

2. Determine the date, time, and place of the next group meeting.

3. Close in prayer.

Chapter Three: Prayer and Conflict

– *Summarize*

Facilitator: initiate this meeting by talking about the idea of praying when you would rather not be praying. Lead the team in a discussion of the difference between *efficient prayers vs. effective prayers.* If you are going to pray effective prayers as a group, what kind of prayers might you be praying for your situation?

– *Discussion*

1. The author spends a significant amount of time teaching on the sanctifying role of prayer (see the section *"The Specific Role of Prayer"* in this chapter).

2. Consider together the idea of the potential impact of sanctifying prayer on your particular situation. What are the possibilities of change that the Lord might want to bring about in your ministry setting if you are willing to be patient in His presence and willing to listen to what He desires? Discuss this long enough to collectively have a clear sense of where this is leading.

3. Take time at this point to discuss the two passages considered in the book on principles: patience and perseverance.

4. How might the practice of these two biblical principles of prayer impact your ministry setting? Have each member of the group share how he or she would grade the leadership team on the carrying out these two prayer principles in your ministry setting.

– *Prayer*

1. Plan to get together as a group for the sole purpose of praying. This will be your next group meeting.

2. Commit to praying for patience, but be determined to continue to pray until God begins to reveal to the entire group what He desires for you as a leadership team in regard to your concerns.

3. This may mean that the group will be in a "tread water" stage until God speaks a common message to all involved in the leadership team. It will test your willingness and commitment to being patient and your perseverance.

4. Once a sense of direction is realized among the group, gather back together to reevaluate where you are in the development of a plan for addressing the conflict that exists in your ministry setting.

– *Closing*

1. Capture verbally and in writing what you believe God is saying through His Word and in your hearts and minds about how the church should address or prepare in your attempt to move toward resolution.

2. Once this is clear, set the next date, time, and place of your meeting.

3. Close your meeting in prayer.

Chapter Four: Jesus, Paul, and Difficult People

– *Summarize*

1. Facilitator: bring to the attention of the group the importance of having a strategy for responding to conflict that is consistent with the lifestyle pattern of Christ.

2. The author states that there are two New Testament passages (Matthew 18:15–20 and 2 Corinthians 2:5–11) that are most helpful in guiding our thoughts regarding conflict in the church, especially conflict that involves difficult people. Take time now, as a group, to study these passages and glean from them, guided by the book, insights that will be helpful to you as you further develop your strategy.

– *Discussion*

1. It was suggested by the author that *reconciliation* (Matthew 18:15–20) is a primary ingredient involved in completing an effective plan of dealing with conflict. As a group, review your thoughts thus far in this study guide and determine whether or not and to what degree this element is included in your strategy.

2. If you discover that your strategy is missing these key elements, consider how you might revise your thoughts to include these biblical concepts

3. After thinking about what Jesus says concerning reconciliation, the apostle Paul teaches on the crucial work of bringing the reconciliation to the desired end that is called *restoration* (w Corinthians 2:5–11). As a group, read this text and talk about how the church was instructed to behave once the man had been reconciled. How might this be instructive for the church today that wants to bring any conflict to full resolution?

– *Prayer*

1. No plan is complete without committing the plan to the Lord. Spend some quality time right now in prayer asking God to give you peace about what you have learned, and decided to do in terms of a proactive plan for responding to conflict of any kind in your ministry setting.

– *Closing*

1. The final step in this process is to agree on a clearly defined plan of action as leaders. Spend time talking about what you have learned, and articulate as best you can the essentials of what God has taught you through this process.

2. After the group has agreed on the basics of the plan for resolving conflict as a church, spend time having one person put this plan into writing. Between now and the final meeting of the group, have the written copy distributed to every group member so he or she can read it and make final comments. At the final meeting, discuss the document and agree on its final form.

3. Spend some valuable time in prayer over the plan that is now in writing.

4. Plan the date, time, and place of the final meeting.

5. Set a date in the future for a six-month review of the plan. Use this opportunity to determine whether or not the plan continues to be the appropriate, and agreed upon a way for resolving conflict in the life of the church.

6. Close the meeting in prayer.

Appendix:
Selected Annotated Bibliography

Anderson, James D. and Ezra Earl Jones. *The Management of Ministry*. San Francisco, CA: Harper and Row, 1978.

> *What is the key to managing the church? Anderson and Jones believe that the "authenticity" of the pastor is of primary importance in dealing with the "dilemmas" of the ministry. The authors take a close look at the leadership of the pastor.*

Armstrong, William H. *Minister, Heal Thyself*. New York, NY: The Pilgrim Press, 1985.

> *A pastor's best option in dealing with difficult people might be to ask, "Am I my most difficult person and God's too!" This book takes a good and close look at many of the difficult times and experiences in the ministry. Experiences like loneliness, failure, rejection, and disappointment to name a few.*

Bell, Donald A. *How to Get Along With People in the Church*. Grand Rapids, MI: Zondervan Publishing Co., 1960.

> *Why are some leaders more effective than others? Bell suggests insights through the example of Jesus, principles of applied psychology, and the psychology of salesmanship. According to*

Bell, understanding people (Bell offers ten suggestions) is the key task before leadership, particularly as it relates to conflict resolution.

Berkley, James D. *Called Into Crisis*. Waco, TX: Word Book Publishing, 1989.

The ability to handle a crisis is predetermined largely by the identification of a potential crisis. Berkley offers thoughts both on identification and the proper handling of a crisis.

Biersdorf, John E. *How Prayer Shapes Ministry*. Washington, DC: The Alban Institute, Inc., 1992.

Biersdorf takes a close look at the way prayer shapes the ministry for the leader of today. This is difficult at times to follow, but it nevertheless contains some very helpful material for the leader who wants to take a closer look at the way prayer changes things in the ministry, especially the one who prays.

Bossart, Donald E. *Creative Conflict in Religious and Church Administration*. Birmingham, AL: Religious Education Press, 1980.

Conflict is viewed as a multifaceted dimension of the pastoral ministry. Dynamics such as the psychological, sociological, and theological aspects of conflict are discussed.

Bramson, Robert M. *Coping with Difficult People*. Garden City, NJ: Anchor Press, Doubleday, 1981.

Each person who faces conflict has a particular style of coping. Bramson offers insight on finding your style and understanding the coping style of others.

Buzzard, Lynn R. and Laurence Eck. *Tell It To The Church*. Elgin, IL: David C. Cook, 1982.

> *Buzzard and Eck discuss a three-step path to fulfilling the admonition of Matthew 18. The authors borrow a model of Kraybill's eight ways to keep a disagreement going. This offers a unique slant on understanding conflict resolution.*

Cavanaugh, Michael E. *The Effective Minister: Psychological and Social Considerations*. San Francisco, CA: Harper and Row, 1986.

> *Helpful insight into the qualities and characteristics of effective pastoral leadership are discussed. A unique contribution is made in this area of study by looking at the role of prayer in conflict, the process of taking a pastoral inventory, and evaluation of the parish as well as offering meditations for the pastor.*

Cedar, Paul; Kent Hughes; and Ben Patterson. *Mastering the Pastoral Role*. Portland, OR: Multnomah Press, 1991.

> *The pastor is seen in this book as the one who establishes a vision for the church. The reader will find helpful discussions on developing a balance between the pastor's strengths and weaknesses while leading. There is an emphasis on leadership and relationships in this material.*

Cohen, William A. *The Art of the Leader*. Englewood, NJ: Prentice Hall, 1990.

> *The author presents some interesting and perhaps unusual approaches to leadership (i.e., the combat model). Strategies are offered for becoming effective leaders as well as steps to assist the leader in facing a crisis situation.*

Cousins, Doug; Keith Anderson, and Arthur DeKruyter. *Mastering Church Management*. Portland, OR: Multnomah Press, 1991.

> *Proper management of any ministry involves a satisfactory stewardship of power. These authors discuss this important and oftentimes potent subject in terms of relationships. Ultimately, they offer some useful steps toward the proper stewardship of power. This work also includes a helpful look at the process of changes within the church.*

Covey, Stephen R. *The 7 Habits of Highly Effective People*. New York, NY: A Fireside Book, 1989.

> *Covey offers many helpful thoughts about being an effective leader. His most powerful and useful tool is his emphasis on being principle-centered. A book well worth reading by every leader.*

Dale, Robert D. *Surviving Difficult Church Members*. Nashville, TN: Abingdon Press, 1984.

> *Models of conflict management are offered by Dale, as well as some helpful insights into the process of identifying the "difficult person" and his or her strategy of creating conflict points in the church setting.*

Dobson, G. Edward, Speed B. Leas, and Marshall Shelley. *Mastering Conflict & Controversy*. Portland, OR: Multnomah Press, 1992.

> *These three veterans of the ministry address a variety of subjects in this new book on dealing with conflict. They speak to subjects such as "maintaining confidence in conflict" and "restoring a fallen brother." Other subjects are included in this helpful book on conflict resolution that are worth further study by any leader.*

Edwards, Gene and Tom Brandon. *Preventing a Church Split*. Scarborough, ME: Christian Books, 1937.

> *Helpful material provided on conflict management, especially in terms of prevention, reconciliation, and responding to conflict and crisis situations.*

Edwards, Judson. *What They Never Told Us ... About How to Get Along With Each Other*. Eugene, OR: Harvest House Publishers, 1991.

> *This book is a real delight to read. It contains many powerful insights into the task of dealing with a difficult person, especially Edward's concept of "tender collisions."*

Fairfield, G.T. James. *When You Don't Agree*. Scottsdale, PA: Herald Press, 1977.

> *The strength of Fairfield's book is in its ability to help a leader identify his/her own conflict style. By doing this, Fairfield assists the leader in his/her own understanding of how best to approach a particular conflict through being able to envision the results of a particular action.*

Fenton, Jr., Horace L. *When Christians Clash: How to Prevent and Resolve the Pain of Conflict*. Downer's Grove, IL: InterVarsity Press, 1987.

> *Fenton focuses on the task of confrontation in the conflict resolution process. He offers special discussion on doctrine as the reason for conflict in the church ministry setting.*

Gerig, Donald. *Leadership in Crisis*. Ventura, CA: Regal Books, 1981.

> *A worthwhile look at the relationship between leadership and humility. Diversity, equality, and differences are central topics of discussion in this useful book on leadership.*

Giblin, Les. *How to Have Confidence and Power in Dealing with People.* New York, NY: The Benjamin Company, Inc., 1956.

> *This book is a little out of the norm for those dealing with this subject. Giblin addresses the matter of conflict resolution primarily from the point of view that believes you can get what you want out of a difficult person by using the right words, etc., in order to get the person on your side. It borders on subtle manipulation; however, Giblin offers enough helpful insights into this subject matter that he is worth reading.*

Hansel, Tim. *Eating Problems for Breakfast.* Dallas, TX: Word Publishing, 1988.

> *This is a very helpful book for the leader who lacks creativity. Hansel provides a very insightful look at the role of creativity in problem solving.*

Haugk, Kenneth. *Antagonists in the Church: How to Identify and Deal with Destructive Conflict.* Minneapolis, MN: Augsburg Publishing House, 1988.

> *Haugk's major contribution in this book is his discussion of the red flags of antagonism. His work on identification the antagonists in your context is extremely helpful.*

Hinkle, James and Tim Woodroof. *Among Friends: You Can Make Your Church a Warmer Place.* Colorado, Springs, CO: NAVPRESS, 1989.

> *These authors provide an interesting look at the task of conflict resolution. Most helpful in their presentation is chapter nine (Heart to Heart Combat), which deals with the strengths and weaknesses of the most common reactions to conflict.*

Hodnett, Edward. *The Art of Problem Solving: How to Improve Your Methods.* New York, NY: Harper & Row Publishers, 1955.

> *Hodnett offers the reader a systematic approach to problem solving that is especially helpful for those leaders with a leaning toward the logical approach to solving conflict.*

Hunter, W. Bingham. *The God Who Hears.* Downer's Grove, IL: InterVarsity Press, 1986.

> *Hunter looks at prayer through the lens of God's character, especially His Sovereignty. He also provides an interesting discussion of the Lord's Prayer. One highlight of Hunters' book is an appendix that deals with the scriptures and prayer.*

Huttenlocker, Keith. *Conflict and Caring: Preventing, Managing and Resolving Conflict in the Church.* Grand Rapids, MI: Zondervan Publishing Co., 1988.

> *Insightful discussion on the emotions and mentality of conflict are provided in this work. Huttenlocker provides brief but helpful material on various options or approaches used in dealing with conflict.*

Hybels, Bill. *Too Busy Not to Pray: Slowing Down to Be with God.* Downer's Grove, IL: InterVarsity Press, 1988.

> *Very well written and extremely practical. Perhaps the best contribution is Hybel's treatment of things that block prayer (prayer busters). His chapter on listening to God is also well worth reading for every pastor.*

Kesler, Jay. *Being Holy, Being Human.* Waco, TX: Word 4 Books, 1988.

> *The pastoral ministry is filled with frustration and joy. The effective pastor must learn to balance his ministry between these two experiences. Kesler helps the reader distinguish between realistic and unrealistic expectations in the ministry. A close*

look at where expectations come from and what they are is an integral part of this work.

Killinger, John. *Christ in the Season of Ministry.* Waco, TX: Word Books, 1981.

> *If you've ever wanted to quit, then this book is for you. Killinger takes a close look at the phases of the ministry, with a particular focus on failure. He offers a positive look at Peter's transhistorical experiences of failure.*

King, Michael A. "The Lame Duck Becomes a Swan." *The Other Ministry* 21 (1990): 8–10.

> *Leaving a ministry can produce a great variety of emotions that must be worked through on a personal level. This is particularly true should you leave due to conflict. King offers some helpful ideas on how to process these kinds of emotions once you decide to leave.*

Kreider, Alan. "Rules for Debating Enemies." *The Other Side* 26 (Jan–Feb. 1990): 6–18.

> *Useful guidelines are provided for the task of communicating with those who hold to opposing viewpoints. Kreider discusses the weaknesses of debating when seeking to work through conflicting views.*

Larson, Bruce; Paul Anderson; and Doug Self. *Mastering Pastoral Care.* Portland, OR: Multnomah Press, 1990.

> *An interesting idea is proposed in this book. Visitation is seen as a possible means of averting oncoming crisis situations.*

Leas, Speed. *Bibliography of Conflict Counseling.* New York, NY: Alban Institute Publication, 1990.

> *Speed Leas provides a helpful list of resources for the process of conflict counseling. This list contains some books not included in this bibliography. Between the two lists, a leader will find many useful resources for effective management of conflict.*

_____. *Discover Your Conflict Management Style.* New York, NY: Alban Institute Publication, 1984.

> *This tool will assist the interested leader in the work of identifying his or her particular style of conflict management. This work is clear and easy to read/understand.*

_____. *Moving Your Church Through Conflict.* New York, NY: Alban Institute Publication, 1991.

> *This is a very useful tool for the pastor/leader who needs help in working through a conflict with his or her church. Most helpful in this book is the identification of "Special Problems in the Church."*

Leas, Speed and Paul Kittlaus. *Church Fights: Managing Conflict in the Local Church.* Philadelphia, PA: Westminster Press, 1973.

> *Discussions on the role of an objective third party (referee; sometimes the pastor) when dealing with conflict. Leas and Kittlaus offer many helpful tools (i.e., questionnaires, surveys, interviews, etc.) that can be used in working out problems in the church.*

Littauer, Francis. *How to Get Along with Difficult People.* Eugene, OR: Harvest House Publishers, 1984

> *Littauer provides some helpful information in her book about identifying the difficult person. She offers much insight into the temperaments and patterns of operation usually associated with*

the difficult person. Her biblical studies of Paul and his dealings with people in conflict is also insightful and helpful.

Littauer, Francis. *Personality Plus: How to Understand Others By Understanding Yourself.* Tarrytown, NY: Fleming H. Revell Publishers, 1983.

> *Littauer again looks at leadership and conflict resolution through the lens of personality and temperament traits. The most helpful contribution of this book is the Personality Profile Test provided by Littauer.*

Matthew, Dewitt. *Capers of the Ministry.* Grand Rapids, MI: Baker Book House, 1976.

> *Working with disgruntled people is part of the ongoing work of the ministry. Matthew presents some helpful thoughts on how the clergy and laity can work together, even in the midst of conflict. The strength of this work is the author's concise comments on issues that arise in the everyday ministry of the church.*

McKenna, David L. *Renewing Our Ministry.* Waco, TX: Word Books, 1986.

> *Mckenna provides information on the role of stress when dealing with conflict. Subjects such as burnout and the prevention of burnout are discussed. The matter of servanthood is also seen as a key to working through any type of conflict. McKenna uses the scripture as the basis for his analysis of conflict management. This is a strength of this work.*

McSwain, Larry L., and William C. Treadwell. *Conflict Ministry in the Church.* Nashville, TN: Broadman Press, 1981.

> *The emphasis of this work is on the processes of conflict development and conflict management. A special asset of this work is the provision of assessment tools to be used in conflict resolution. The authors also provide insight into the role of stress in conflict and the difficult task of working with "stressed out" people.*

Miller, Keith. *Secrets of Staying Power.* Philadelphia, PA: Westminster Press, 1978,

> *What pastor has not faced the experience of being discouraged in the ministry? Miller provides insight into the major contributors of discouragement. Facing a difficult person (a source of discouragement) in the ministry can lead to discouragement. Miller offers survival strategies that can be used when dealing with your difficult person.*

Moeller, Robert. "Pastor David or Pastor Solomon?" *Christianity Today* 10 (Winter 1989): 104–109.

> *Good biblical insight into the matter of church conflict via the metaphor of two character studies: David and Solomon.*

Muck, Terry. *When to Take a Risk: Guide to Pastoral Decision Making.* Waco, TX: Word Books, 1987.

> *To be an effective leader one must take certain risks, says Terry Muck. Various kinds of risks are addressed by Muck, as well as the reasons why leaders are reluctant to take risks. Muck offers a risk "profile" sheet with answers that could prove helpful for any leader facing such a decision.*

Myra, Harold (ed.). *Leaders: Learning Leadership from Some of Christianity's Best* (The Leadership Library). Carol Stream, IL: Word Books, 1987.

> *With a special emphasis on maintaining integrity under pressure and proper evaluation of one's performance, Myra offers helpful insights into how a leader can understand his or her personal role in a ministry setting.*

Noblett, Robert A. "Is Conflict Always Bad?" *The Christian Ministry* 21 (1990): 11–13.

> *Conflict is not always bad, writes Noblett. The church can and will have creative and redemptive conflict. Noblett, using*

scripture as a basis of understanding, examines the balance between peace and conflict in the life of Jesus and offers suggestions on how we can model his example.

Oglesby, Robert K. "Grinning Down Bears." *Leadership* 10 (Winter 1989): 24–25.

> *Central to the discussion in this article is the task of neutralizing the difficult person. Oglesby provides some helpful steps toward disarmament when facing potential conflict with a person. He is careful to avoid manipulation.*

Osborne, Larry W. *The Unity Factor: Getting Your Church Leaders to Work Together*. Carol Stream, IL: Word Books, 1989.

> *The basic thesis of Osborne's work is the idea that the pursuit of unity must be the priority in the church. Suggesting that most church fights are not over theology but priorities, he provides three key ingredients to unity that must be pursued.*

Pratt, Richard L. *Pray with Your Eyes Open*. Phillipsburg, NJ: Presbyterian and Reformed Publishing Company, 1987.

> *Pratt offers solid thought on the importance of communication in prayer. He also brings to print a helpful look at prayer offered in various types of situations and needs.*

Rauch, Gerry. *Handling Conflict: Taking the Tension Out of Difficult Relationships*. Ann Arbor, MI: Servant Books, 1985.

> *The key to conflict resolution, states Rauch, is to know what the conflict is all about. Once we understand the personalities involved as well as the preferences of the key people, resolution is possible. The book is helpful in knowing how to proceed in reaching resolution of a given conflict.*

Rush, Myron. *Burnout: Practical Help for Lives Out of Balance*. Wheaton, IL: Victor Books, 1987.

> *Rush offers an interesting thesis in this book. He suggests that burnout is partially caused by excessive dealings with the problems of other people or problem people. The book's strength is the discussion of factors leading to burnout and what might be done about them.*

Shelley, Marshall. *Helping Those Who Don't Want Help*. Waco, TX: Word Books, 1986.

> *There are all kinds of difficult people in the church of today. However, identifying them is another story. Shelley provides some invaluable insight and assistance in completing this task. Once identified, Shelley gives specific strategies that can be used to deal properly with the difficult person. He also speaks openly about what to do when nothing seems to work.*

Smith, Fred. *Learning to Lead*. Waco, TX: Word Books, 1986.

> *What is a leader? What does a leader do? Smith looks at this important subject through the question of motivation and the abuse of it (sometimes of manipulation). A special feature of this book is the author's look at the invisible side of leadership and the rewards of leadership.*

Spickelmier, Jim. "Spittin' Out Peas: When the Question is Control." *Christianity Today* 10 (Spring 1989):118ff

> *Traditional methods of intervention into conflict situations are not always adequate. Conflict resolution is particularly tied into effective leadership. The thesis of this article is that the continuity of leadership in the church is critical.*

Swindoll, Charles R. *Hand Me Another Brick*. Nashville, TN: Thomas Nelson, 1990.

> *Leadership comes from the rank and file, argues Swindoll. However, this person must be highly motivated. Swindoll, in his normal fashion, offers a fascinating study of leadership through the eyes of Nehemiah, a well-known Old Testament leader. He provides some wonderful insight into the role of prayer in the development of a leader and the accomplishment of the leader's task. This book could be used as a bible study and guide to dealing with opposition.*

Tirabassi, Becky. *Let Prayer Change Your Life*. Nashville, TN: Thomas Nelson Publishers, 1990.

> *Tirabassi's discussion of the way prayer changes people, especially the leader, is very helpful. Perhaps her best contribution in this book is her treatment of prayer principles (chapter 8).*

Underwood, Ralph L. *Empathy and Confrontation in Pastoral Care*. Philadelphia, PA: Fortress Press, 1985.

> *Confronting people in crisis situations can be tough. It is extremely hard to be empathetic at times, but Underwood offers some helpful ideas on the development of an empathetic spirit. He focuses on the importance of the role of respect when involved in confrontation, yet he moves beyond empathy to using confrontation as a tool for personal growth.*

Wetherwax, John R. "Holding Your Ground." *Leadership* 9 (Spring 1988): 114–118.

> *This article suggests that conflict is a given. It should be expected, so pick your battles carefully and hold your ground. Wetherwax argues that convictions are okay and that what is needed is proper ways to work with those who hold different viewpoints and opinions so that conflict does not take place and produce division.*

Willimon, William H. *Preaching About Conflict in the Local Church.* Philadelphia, PA: The Westminster Press, 1987.

> *Willimon addresses the subject of conflict from an interesting perspective. He looks at conflict through the eyes of the pastor whose primary task in the local church is to preach. This book deals effectively with the topic of preaching the controversial sermon.*